Vikings

Unleash Your Inner Warrior for Leadership Success

(An Enthralling Journey of Exploration to Uncover the Secrets of the Vikings)

Glenn Lowery

Published By **Darby Connor**

Glenn Lowery

Vikings: Unleash Your Inner Warrior for Leadership Success (An Enthralling Journey of Exploration to Uncover the Secrets of the Vikings)

ISBN 978-0-9953324-6-1

Legal & Disclaimer

The information contained in this book is not designed to replace or take the place of any form of medicine or professional medical advice. The information in this book has been provided for educational & entertainment purposes only.

The information contained in this book has been compiled from sources deemed reliable, and it is accurate to the best of the Author's knowledge; however, the Author cannot guarantee its accuracy and validity and cannot be held liable for any errors or omissions. Changes are periodically made to this book. You must consult your doctor or get professional medical advice before using any of the suggested remedies, techniques, or information in this book.

Upon using the information contained in this book, you agree to hold harmless the Author from and against any damages, costs, and expenses, including any legal fees potentially resulting from the application of any of the information provided by this guide. This disclaimer applies to any damages or injury caused by the use and application, whether directly or indirectly, of any advice or information presented, whether for breach of contract, tort, negligence, personal injury, criminal intent, or under any other cause of action.

You agree to accept all risks of using the information presented inside this book. You need to consult a professional medical practitioner in order to ensure you are both able and healthy enough to participate in this program.

Table Of Contents

Chapter 1: Viking Astrology

In the nation-states of Norse mythology, in which gods and goddesses reign outstanding and the threads of destiny are intricately woven, lies the fascinating international of Viking Astrology. Unlike the Western zodiac, which you'll be acquainted with, Norse astrology offers a very precise and profound attitude at the celestial forces that shape our lives. Prepare to embark on a adventure of self-discovery as we discover the secrets and techniques and techniques and techniques of the Norse runes and the customized nature of the Norse zodiac.

To recognize the roots of Viking Astrology, we need to first immerse ourselves within the massive and fascinating tapestry of Norse mythology. At its middle, Norse mythology is a rich series of historic memories that show the beliefs and values of the Norse human beings. It paints a glittery photograph of a international populated with the useful resource of gods, giants, elves, and one of a kind mystical beings, every gambling a tremendous characteristic inside the complicated net of life.

Astrology, in Norse mythology, is deeply intertwined with the concept of the Norns, the effective and enigmatic weavers of future. These 3 divine beings, referred to as Urðr (the past), Verðandi (the triumphing), and Skuld (the future), non-public an exquisite records of the tapestry of existence. Their problematic art work, guided via the Allfather Odin, determines the future of anybody.

Central to the Norns' mastery is the concept of the thread of destiny. This ethereal thread connects each being, from the mightiest gods to the humblest mortals, to the tapestry of life. It represents the interaction amongst loose will and the predetermined, the choices we make and the path that future has woven for us.

Understanding the thread of future is crucial to comprehending the profound insights that Viking Astrology gives.

At the coronary coronary coronary heart of Viking Astrology lies the sacred language of the runes. The runes, historic symbols steeped in mystery and strength, feature the keys that free up the understanding and steering of the gods. Their origins may be traced decrease returned to the Allfather himself, Odin, who released right into a momentous quest to discover their secrets and techniques.

According to fable, Odin hung himself from the powerful World Tree, Yggdrasil, sacrificing himself to the unknown in pursuit of expertise. For 9 nights, he continued the ache and struggling, looking into the depths of the cosmic mysteries. It changed into in the course of this perilous ordeal that the runes, whispered to him via the very material of the universe, were positioned.

Odin's sacrifice symbolizes the transformative power of facts and the deep connection a number of the gods and mortal nation-states. Through his selfless act, he not satisfactory received mastery over the runes but furthermore bestowed upon humanity the functionality to get right of entry to their profound data.

Within the tough language of the runes lies a customized zodiac that presentations the individual and future of every person. This unique issue units Viking Astrology aside from its Western counterpart. Instead of twelve signs and symptoms, the Norse zodiac encompasses twenty-4 runes, every sporting its own awesome power and symbolism.

To in reality hold near the know-how of Viking Astrology, one should engage with the runes on a personal diploma. Each individual is born underneath the have an effect on of a sun rune, which exhibits the overarching issue matters that form their destiny. The date of delivery performs a crucial position in identifying this solar rune and its profound importance in an person's life.

Additionally, the start hour rune further refines the cosmic energies imprinted upon an character at the time of their transport. By statistics the shipping hour rune, one gains valuable insights into the precise impacts that shape their character, strengths, and stressful situations.

Throughout our adventure, we can discover each rune in-intensity, unraveling their secrets and unlocking their strength. From the financial wealth rune, Fehu, to the intuitive and modern rune, Kenaz, every photo holds a wealth of recognition that can be harnessed to navigate lifestyles's complexities.

Practical guidance will accompany our exploration of the runes, allowing you to contain their energy into your lifestyles. By embracing the knowledge of the runes, you may cultivate electricity, resilience, instinct, stability, and protection. You will discover ways to embody trade, nurture relationships, discover delight inside the easy pleasures, and boom the patience and expertise to triumph over demanding situations.

As we embark on this great voyage into the depths of Viking Astrology, I urge you to approach this historical expertise with an open coronary heart and a willingness to explore the unknown. By embracing the personalized nature of the Norse zodiac and the profound insights furnished thru the runes, you could discover the hidden threads that be a part of you to the gods and your truest self.

In the chapters that comply with, we are able to journey thru the geographical regions of myth and magic, guided thru the expertise of the Norns and the electricity of the runes. Prepare to find out the transformative ability that lies within your very very own transport runes and encompass the harmonious dance between destiny and unfastened will. As you immerse your self in the pages of "Viking Astrology: Unveiling the Secrets of the Norse Runes," might also additionally moreover you embark on a profound and empowering path of self-discovery and personal increase.

The Norns and the Thread of Fate

In the geographical regions of Norse mythology, the Norns stand as effective and mysterious beings, weaving the hard tapestry of destiny itself. To apprehend the essence of Viking Astrology and its connection to the cosmic forces that shape our lives, we must discover the feature of those divine weavers and the idea of the thread of future.

The Norns, Urðr, Verðandi, and Skuld, are the daughters of the primordial large, Ymir.

They preserve huge electricity and data, reputation because the guardians and arbiters of destiny. Urðr, whose call approach "past," governs the occasions that have already spread out. Verðandi, the "gift," holds sway over the present day circumstances. Lastly, Skuld, the "destiny," determines the effects however to come back.

These 3 effective sisters, with their profound information of the intricacies of existence, sit down under the substantial World Tree, Yggdrasil. It is right right here that they spin and form the threads of fate, guiding the destinies of gods, mortals, and all beings alike.

Central to the Norns' mastery is the concept of the thread of destiny. This airy thread, woven with the useful resource in their skilled fingers, connects all residing beings, binding them together in an tough tapestry. It symbolizes the interaction amongst loose will and the predetermined, the selections we make and the route that future has laid earlier than us.

To in truth admire the importance of the thread of destiny, we should understand its significance in Viking astrology. It serves as the foundation upon which the runes are interpreted, imparting insights into an character's individual, strengths, and disturbing situations. The thread of destiny intertwines with the energies of the runes, guiding humans alongside their precise paths.

Within the Norse zodiac, each rune represents a first-rate strength and symbolism. When blended with the thread of destiny, the ones runes offer a custom designed roadmap of an character's adventure thru existence. The Norns, with their profound knowledge of the beyond, gift, and destiny, imbue the runes with their attention and insights.

As we embark on our exploration of the runes in the following chapters, it's far critical to recognize the sacred bond many of the Norns, the thread of destiny, and the cosmic forces that form our lifestyles. By statistics this problematic interaction, we benefit a deeper appreciation for the profound insights and steering furnished via Viking Astrology.

Practical Points:

Reflect at the concept of future: Take a 2nd to contemplate the concept of destiny and free will in your private lifestyles. Consider the alternatives you have were given made and the techniques in which your route may had been inspired with the aid of using outdoor forces. Recognize that, honestly due to the reality the Norns weave the thread of destiny, you own the energy to form your private future.

Embrace the interconnectedness of all beings: The thread of future reminds us of the interconnectedness of all dwelling subjects. Consider the impact of your actions on others and the arena round you. Nurture compassion and empathy, spotting that the options you are making ripple thru the tapestry of existence.

Seek knowledge from the beyond, gift, and future: The Norns encompass the expertise of the past, gift, and destiny. Learn from the reports of folks who came in advance than you, live mindfully in the gift, and embody the functionality of what's yet to come returned. Seek steering from numerous property, drawing at the collective statistics of generations.

Reflect on the threads of your private life: Take time to mirror at the sports and tales that have fashioned your adventure up to now. Recognize the significance of each tough and joyous moments, facts that every thread contributes to the complicated tapestry of your existence.

Embrace the interconnectedness of Viking Astrology: As we delve deeper into the runes, do not forget the interconnectedness of Viking Astrology. The Norns, the thread of future, and the runes themselves are intertwined, providing profound insights into your man or woman and future. Embrace the holistic nature of this historical understanding, understanding that each trouble informs and enhances the others.

By embracing the know-how of the Norns and the thread of fate, you open yourself to a deeper records of the profound insights furnished through Viking Astrology. As we maintain our journey via the chapters that observe, we're able to get to the bottom of the secrets and techniques and techniques of the individual runes and the transformative capacity they hold. Prepare to embark on a route of self-discovery and empowerment, guided through the records of the Norns and the cosmic forces that shape our life.

Odin's Quest for the Runes

In the full-size tapestry of Norse mythology, few testimonies captivate the imagination as intensely as Odin's quest for the runes. This mythological tale unravels the origins of the runes, their profound significance, and the transformative adventure of self-discovery undertaken with the resource of the use of the Allfather himself.

The tale starts offevolved with Odin, the smart and enigmatic ruler of the Aesir gods. Seeking to free up the secrets of the cosmos and acquire the eye held in the runes, Odin released into a deadly adventure of self-sacrifice and enlightenment.

High above the geographical areas of mortals and gods, Odin ventured to the vicinity tree, Yggdrasil. A towering and majestic presence, Yggdrasil prolonged its branches at some degree within the heavens, on the equal time as its roots delved deep into the geographical regions of the underworld. Here, under the incredible cover of Yggdrasil, Odin sought the steerage of the Norns, the weavers of future.

Driven through his insatiable thirst for statistics, Odin pierced his very private aspect together together with his powerful spear, Gungnir. As blood poured from his wound, he suspended himself from the branches of Yggdrasil, sacrificing himself to the unknown in an act of first rate devotion.

For 9 nights and days, Odin hung in pain, his imaginative and prescient blurred via way of the ache and darkness. It modified into at some point of this grueling ordeal that the secrets and techniques of the runes commenced out out to show themselves to him. Whispers from the very material of the universe, the runes whispered their popularity and insights to the Allfather, their strength flowing into his being.

As Odin teetered on the precipice of existence and loss of life, the sacrifice he made bore fruit. The runes, every sporting its very personal precise electricity and symbolism, have grow to be etched upon his interest. Through his unwavering willpower and selflessness, Odin had obtained the expertise and understanding that would form the future of gods and mortals alike.

The significance of Odin's quest for the runes lies not extremely good in the acquisition of records but also inside the transformative strength of sacrifice. Odin's act of piercing himself with Gungnir and surrendering his physical comfort symbolizes the profound intensity of information and boom that can be attained through sacrifice and perseverance.

Practical Points:

Embrace sacrifice for records: Reflect at the sacrifices you're willing to make in pursuit of understanding, growth, and self-discovery. Understand that genuine transformation frequently calls for stepping out of your comfort quarter and embracing demanding situations.

Seek expertise with an open thoughts: Like Odin, approach the pursuit of knowledge with an open thoughts and a willingness to discover the unknown. Be receptive to new thoughts, numerous perspectives, and insights from surprising assets. Cultivate a thirst for records that transcends obstacles.

Persevere thru stressful conditions: Odin's 9-night time time ordeal placing from Yggdrasil symbolizes the importance of perseverance within the face of disturbing conditions. Embrace difficult situations as opportunities for boom and self-discovery. Stay committed on your path, although it feels overwhelming or uncertain.

Embody self-sacrifice for a more motive: Consider the processes in which you can exercising self-sacrifice for the betterment of yourself and others. This ought to include letting circulate of personal dreams for the gain of a larger aim, presenting help to those in need, or devoting time and effort to a worth cause.

Reflect on the electricity of transformation: Odin's quest for the runes serves as a reminder of the transformative strength of expertise and self-discovery. Take time to mirror on your non-public journey of boom and the methods wherein acquiring new insights has unique your lifestyles. Embrace the ongoing approach of transformation and allow the statistics of the runes to manual you.

As we keep our exploration of Viking Astrology and the runes that shape its basis, endure in thoughts Odin's sacrifice and the information he won. The runes, infused alongside collectively together with his transformative journey, deliver the electricity to mild up our paths, shape our destinies, and empower us to include the depths of our actual ability. Open yourself to the commands and insights that sit up straight for in the chapters beforehand, and embark in your non-public quest for self-discovery and enlightenment.

Chapter 2: The Solar

In the sizable cosmic tapestry of Viking Astrology, the Solar Rune stands as a radiant beacon, illuminating the course of one's destiny. Symbolizing the power and power bestowed upon us with the aid of way of the solar, the Solar Rune holds profound significance in figuring out an man or woman's future based totally totally on their date of delivery. By records the essence of the Solar Rune and its interaction with the celestial forces, we will unlock a deeper information of ourselves and our existence's motive.

The Solar Rune, also called Sól, represents the divine have an effect on of the solar, which holds a important position in Norse cosmology. Just because the solar brings warmth, slight, and existence to the place, the Solar Rune shines its guiding moderate upon our lifestyles, revealing our innate strengths, competencies, and the course that awaits us.

Each Solar Rune corresponds to a particular date of shipping and consists of its own specific electricity and symbolism. By analyzing the Solar Rune associated with our starting date, we gain belief into the middle components of our man or woman and the tendencies that shape our adventure via life.

Practical Points:

Discover your Solar Rune: Use the appendix system furnished in this ebook, which includes the Rune Charts and Birth Rune Calculator, to decide your Solar Rune. Knowing your Solar Rune will feature a basis for exploring your specific individual traits and understanding how they intertwine with the celestial forces.

Reflect in your strengths and abilities: Once you have got identified your Solar Rune, take time to mirror on the characteristics associated with it. Consider how those strengths and abilities appear in your lifestyles and the manner you could further boom and nurture them. Embrace your innate talents and allow them to manual you inside the route of pleasing your functionality.

Embrace your existence's cause: The Solar Rune famous components of your lifestyles's motive and the path you're destined to walk. Reflect on how your innate characteristics align collectively together with your passions, desires, and aspirations. Take realistic steps to align your existence selections and actions with your motive, permitting the Solar Rune's energy to manual you in the direction of a satisfying and significant lifestyles.

Connect with the energy of the sun: The Solar Rune is in detail connected to the energy of the solar. Take time to bask within the solar's warm temperature rays, whether or not or now not or not it is through spending time outdoors, schooling sun salutations in yoga, or in fact meditating under the sun's moderate glow. Allow the sun's power to infuse you with energy, thought, and a experience of connectedness to the greater cosmos.

Explore your sun rune's historical importance: Delve into the mythology and historic context associated with your Solar Rune. Connect with the ancient expertise and tales associated with your begin rune, letting them deepen your know-how of yourself and your location inside the worldwide.

The Solar Rune serves as a guiding slight, illuminating the particular trends and reason that stay internal every folks. By embracing the facts of the Solar Rune, we're able to navigate our life's journey with readability, self belief, and a deeper records of ourselves. As you preserve your exploration of Viking Astrology, consider the radiance of the Solar Rune and permit it to empower you on your path of self-discovery and success.

The Birth Hour Rune

As we journey deeper into the world of Viking Astrology, we stumble upon a captivating issue that similarly refines our statistics of private future—the Birth Hour Rune. Just because the time of starting is massive in astrology, the hour wherein we input the world holds a unique rune that affects our existence's path and person. The Birth Hour Rune brings forth a nuanced layer of perception, highlighting the complicated tapestry of our lifestyles and providing precious guidance for self-discovery.

The Birth Hour Rune serves as a key that unlocks the secrets and strategies of our individuality, dropping light on the developments, strengths, and annoying conditions that form our lives. It is a mirrored image of the celestial energies gift inside the suggest time we take our first breath, imprinting upon us a totally precise cosmic signature.

Each hour of the day corresponds to a selected rune, representing terrific traits and energies. By exploring the symbolism and interpretations related to the Birth Hour Rune, we're able to gain valuable insights into our innate tendencies, persona developments, and the topics so that you can permeate our lifestyles's adventure.

Practical Points:

Determine your Birth Hour Rune: Utilize the tools furnished inside the appendix, which encompass the Rune Charts and Birth Rune Calculator, to discover your Birth Hour Rune. Understanding this rune will permit you to embark on a deeper exploration of your man or woman and life's route.

Reflect in your inherent traits: Take time to reflect at the traits and developments related to your Birth Hour Rune. Consider how the ones dispositions have manifested in your existence and the way they have got formed your studies and interactions.

Embrace the specific additives of your character and use them as a basis for personal boom and self-recognition.

Recognize the annoying situations and possibilities: Each Birth Hour Rune affords each disturbing conditions and possibilities. Reflect at the ability barriers and strengths associated with your rune, and contemplate how they have got stimulated your existence's journey. Embrace the traumatic situations as possibilities for growth and channel your strengths to navigate them efficaciously.

Embrace the cyclic nature of time: Just because of the truth the hour hand actions in a non-prevent cycle, so too does lifestyles unfold in cycles. Explore the symbolism of your Birth Hour Rune within the context of time's cyclical nature. Consider how the energies represented via way of your rune can also ebb and drift in some unspecified time in the future of unique levels of your life, allowing you to embody change and transformation.

Seek alignment together with your Birth Hour Rune: Embrace the capabilities and energies embodied with the useful useful resource of your Birth Hour Rune and align your existence alternatives and moves therefore. Embracing your rune's symbolism will permit you to stay authentically and in harmony in conjunction with your real nature.

The Birth Hour Rune gives a profound glimpse into the intricacies of our life, providing a deeper information of our innate dispositions and life's troubles. By exploring and honoring the knowledge of this rune, we embark on a adventure of self-discovery, empowerment, and private increase. As you delve into the depths of Viking Astrology, recall the significance of your Birth Hour Rune and permit it to manual you inside the direction of embracing your real self and exciting your particular future.

The Monetary Wealth Rune

In the arena of Viking Astrology, the Fehu rune holds the crucial aspect to know-how our dating with wealth and success. Fehu, often referred to as the Monetary Wealth Rune, goes past cloth possessions and financial earnings. It consists of a holistic mind-set on abundance, encompassing both fabric and religious wealth. Through exploring the depths of Fehu, we get to the bottom of the secrets of prosperity and discover ways to align ourselves with the massive forces of the universe.

At its middle, Fehu represents the power and power required to get up abundance in all areas of lifestyles. It is a rune of motion and initiative, reminding us of our innate power to create the lifestyles we desire. Fehu teaches us that wealth is not totally measured thru possessions but also thru the richness of our studies, relationships, and internal achievement.

Practical Points:

Cultivate a prosperity mindset: Embrace the information that abundance isn't constrained to economic wealth. Shift your recognition inside the route of recognizing and appreciating the abundance already located on your life, inclusive of love, fitness, possibilities, and personal competencies. Cultivate a mind-set of gratitude and abundance, which opens the doors for additonal blessings to circulate your existence.

Take inspired motion: Fehu urges us to achieve this and capture opportunities. Identify your desires and dreams, then create a route of movement to carry them to fruition. Break down your goals into possible steps, and take normal and targeted movement in the path of their attainment. Remember that small, ordinary actions can purpose massive outcomes over time.

Embrace the float of giving and receiving: The Fehu rune emphasizes the significance of balance and reciprocity. Cultivate a healthy relationship with wealth by using the usage of know-how that it is not exceptional about accumulation however additionally approximately sharing and giving lower again. Be generous together with your property, whether or no longer it's time, cash, or competencies, as acts of giving make a contribution to the cycle of abundance.

Assess your values and priorities: Reflect on what simply topics to you and align your financial alternatives together together together with your values. Consider how your spending conduct and financial alternatives replicate your priorities. Intentionally allocate your resources to help the things that carry you joy, boom, and fulfillment. This aware approach to wealth can result in a more super and wealthy existence.

Emphasize self esteem over internet well properly well worth: Fehu teaches us that actual wealth begins offevolved inside. Focus on nurturing your self confidence and internal abundance, recognizing that your price extends beyond fabric possessions. Invest in non-public increase, self-care, and self-improvement. When you cultivate a robust enjoy of self-worth, you lure opportunities and abundance from a place of empowerment.

Seek possibilities for personal growth: Fehu invites us to growth our horizons and capture opportunities for increase and learning. Embrace new tales, acquire new talents, and are attempting to find personal and professional improvement. The pursuit of information and private growth enhances your functionality to take region abundance and opens doorways to new possibilities.

The Fehu rune reminds us that wealth and success are not elusive thoughts however are inside our draw close to on the equal time as we align ourselves with the herbal drift of abundance. By embracing a prosperity mind-set, taking stimulated movement, and spotting the richness in our lives, we invite prosperity to permeate every detail of our life. Embody the electricity of Fehu, harness your creative power, and release the gates to a existence of abundance and success.

Chapter 3: The Strength

In the tapestry of Viking Astrology, the Uruz rune shines as a photograph of private power and resilience. As the Strength Rune, Uruz contains the essence of wild energy and energy. It represents the primal forces of nature and our innate functionality to tap into them. Exploring the depths of Uruz lets in us to harness our inner energy and cultivate the resilience had to face lifestyles's worrying conditions with braveness and resolution.

Uruz reminds us that energy comes in many bureaucracy. It is not confined to bodily prowess however encompasses intellectual, emotional, and non secular fortitude as nicely. This rune calls us to hook up with our primal instincts, having access to the wellspring of power inside us and tapping into our internal reserves of power and determination. By expertise the importance of Uruz, we release the secrets of personal energy and learn how to navigate life's journey with strength and resilience.

Practical Points:

Embrace physical strength: Uruz represents bodily electricity and electricity. Take care of your body by the use of adopting a wholesome manner of lifestyles that includes everyday workout, right vitamins, and enough relaxation. Engage in sports activities that invigorate your frame and build stamina. Explore extraordinary styles of motion consisting of yoga, martial arts, or dance to tap into your bodily electricity and unharness your ability.

Cultivate intellectual and emotional resilience: Uruz teaches us to cultivate internal energy to conquer challenges. Develop intellectual and emotional resilience with the useful resource of working towards mindfulness, meditation, and self-meditated image. Identify and paintings through proscribing beliefs and fears that would save you your personal growth. Embrace traumatic situations as opportunities for increase, studying, and self-discovery. Cultivate a high-quality mind-set and undertake empowering affirmations to strengthen your highbrow and emotional nicely-being.

Embody braveness within the face of adversity: Uruz encourages us to encompass courage at the same time as confronted with obstacles. Take stimulated movement even in the face of worry or uncertainty. Break down demanding situations into functionality steps, and approach them with willpower and perseverance. Trust in your capability to triumph over difficulties, and draw upon your internal strength to navigate through adversity.

Connect with nature's power: Uruz symbolizes our connection to the primal forces of nature. Spend time in nature to recharge and reconnect with the earth's energy. Engage in sports activities including trekking, gardening, or absolutely sitting in contemplation. Allow the natural international to encourage and rejuvenate you, tapping into the incredible power that surrounds us.

Seek possibilities for private increase: Uruz urges us to are looking for private boom and consist of recent opinions. Step out of your comfort area and engage in sports activities that venture you and make bigger your horizons. Pursue mastering opportunities, gather new abilties, or find out innovative stores. By embracing non-public boom, you faucet into your functionality and discover hidden reservoirs of power and resilience.

Support others of their adventure: Uruz moreover reminds us of our capability to help and uplift others. Offer assist, encouragement, and thought to the ones spherical you. Share your research and know-how, performing as a supply of strength for others who can be managing their very own stressful conditions. By fostering a enjoy of network and connection, you make contributions to the collective electricity and resilience of these round you.

The Uruz rune serves as a powerful reminder of our inherent energy and electricity. By embracing the classes of Uruz, we learn how to faucet into our inner reserves of electricity and resilience. Through physical electricity, intellectual and emotional fortitude, and connection with nature, we cultivate a deep wellspring of strength. By embodying braveness and assisting others, we contribute to the collective strength of our companies. Let the Uruz rune manual you on a route of personal empowerment and resilience, allowing you to navigate lifestyles's adventure with unwavering electricity and power.

Thurisaz - The Rune of Thor's Protection

In the giant realm of Viking Astrology, the Thurisaz rune stands as a photo of Thor's powerful safety. As the Rune of Thor's Protection, Thurisaz holds the strength to protect and guide humans in their adventure thru lifestyles. It embodies the protective aspects of Thor, the Norse god of thunder and strength. Exploring the Thurisaz rune allows us to faucet into this divine electricity, presenting us steerage and assist whilst going thru worrying conditions and adversity.

Thurisaz reminds us of the importance of timing and taking movement at the same time as the on the spot is proper. It teaches us to take note of our instincts and act decisively, guided through the know-how of Thor's protection. By know-how the importance of Thurisaz, we release the secrets and techniques and strategies of divine safety and learn how to navigate existence's trials with courage and discernment.

Practical Points:

Trust your instincts: Thurisaz encourages us to accept as authentic with our instincts and internal guidance. Pay attention to your intuition, because it regularly gives precious insights and warnings. Practice quieting your thoughts through meditation or reflected photograph to higher attune yourself for your inner voice. Cultivate a experience of consider in your self and the attention that arises from inside.

Take decisive movement: Thurisaz reminds us that safety requires energetic participation. When confronted with demanding situations, do not forget to your capability to make picks and take appropriate movement. Embrace the braveness to confront boundaries and circulate ahead. By acting decisively, you harness the protective strength of Thurisaz and align yourself with Thor's strength.

Cultivate staying power and timing: While motion is important, Thurisaz moreover emphasizes the importance of staying power and timing. Recognize that now not each state of affairs requires a direct reaction. Allow events to spread clearly, and expect the opportune second to behave. Patience and discernment make sure that your moves are aligned with the protecting energy of Thurisaz.

Seek Thor's protection and guidance: Invoke Thor's safety thru rituals or prayers. Create a sacred place dedicated to Thor or contain Thor's symbols, which includes his hammer Mjölnir, into your non secular practices. Call upon Thor for steerage and strength whilst going via demanding situations or uncertain situations. Trust that his defensive electricity might be with you, supplying manual and encouragement.

Honor the energy of lightning: Lightning is a powerful image related to Thor's would possibly and protection. Connect with the power of lightning through visualization or meditation. Imagine the electric fee coursing via your frame, infusing you with energy and protection. Use this visualization to cultivate resilience and invoke Thor's presence.

Be aware of your surroundings: Thurisaz reminds us to be privy to our environment and capability dangers. Cultivate a experience of vigilance without succumbing to fear. Trust your instincts to manual you a ways from threatening situations. Develop situational popularity and exercising danger assessment to make certain your personal safety.

Act with integrity and honor: Thor is a image of honor and righteousness. Align your self with the ones values for your moves and interactions with others. Act with integrity, treating others with admire and fairness. By embodying those capabilities, you align your self with Thor's defensive energy and entice immoderate quality evaluations into your lifestyles.

Embrace Thor's inclinations: Embrace the traits related to Thor, which incorporates strength, determination, and courage. Engage in physical sports activities that domesticate power and stamina. Embody Thor's fearlessness within the face of adversity, expertise that his shielding strength is with you. Adopt Thor's unwavering willpower to justice and protect what's proper.

The Thurisaz rune offers us the possibility to connect to Thor's protective energy and guidance. By trusting our instincts, taking decisive movement, and cultivating endurance, we align ourselves with the divine protection that Thurisaz represents. By honoring Thor and his symbols, we invite his presence into our lives. By appearing with integrity and embodying Thor's capabilities, we align ourselves alongside along together with his protective power and appeal to fine reminiscences. Embrace the Thurisaz rune, and permit Thor's exceptional protection manual you to your adventure, making sure your safety and strength along the manner.

Ansuz - The Rune of Wisdom

Within the rich tapestry of Viking Astrology, the Ansuz rune shines because the embodiment of records and expertise. Known because the Rune of Wisdom, Ansuz consists of the essence of divine steering and encourages people to are searching for expertise from outdoor belongings. It serves as a reminder of the significance of listening, getting to know, and embracing the insights that smart advocate can provide.

To truely apprehend and harness the power of the Ansuz rune, we want to delve into the realms of facts and knowledge associated with it. By exploring this rune, we open ourselves to the transformative capability of searching out steerage and expanding our knowledge of the area. Let us embark on a journey of discovery and locate the practical steps to embodying the knowledge of Ansuz.

Practical Points:

Seek out mentors and teachers: Embrace the expertise of Ansuz via way of actively seeking out mentors, teachers, or informed individuals who can guide you in your course. Look for experts in fields of interest, be part of test agencies, or engage in publications and workshops that boom your understanding. Embrace the possibility to have a have a look at from the ones who have walked the path in advance than you.

Listen actively: Cultivate the artwork of active listening. When task conversations or receiving steerage, exercise genuinely paying attention to what's being stated. Give your entire hobby, ask insightful questions, and attempting to find to understand the perspectives and opinions of others. By listening attentively, you open yourself to the information that others want to percent.

Read and find out: Immerse yourself in books, articles, and belongings that pertain to subjects of interest or regions you preference to deepen your knowledge in. Seek out genuine belongings and authors who offer nicely-researched statistics and insights. Engage in vital wondering, allowing your realise-how to conform and develop as you discover new thoughts and thoughts.

Reflect and integrate: Wisdom is not honestly obtaining expertise however additionally integrating it into your lifestyles. Take time to mirror on the data you acquire and recollect the way it aligns in conjunction with your values and beliefs. Assess how the expertise you stumble upon may be performed almost to your every day lifestyles, guiding your alternatives and actions.

Embrace numerous perspectives: The know-how of Ansuz invites us to encompass various perspectives and take a look at from a huge sort of property. Seek out viewpoints that venture your very own, mission respectful communicate and communicate. This broadens your information and fosters personal increase, allowing you to cultivate a extra entire perspective.

Connect with ancestral expertise: Tap into the collective interest of your ancestors and cultural ancient beyond. Explore the myths, tales, and traditions of your lineage. Connect with the expertise surpassed down via generations, permitting it to manual and encourage you. By honoring your ancestral statistics, you decorate your own understanding and deepen your connection to the awareness of Ansuz.

Trust your inner knowledge: While looking for outdoor guidance is important, preserve in thoughts to definitely receive as right along with your very personal internal expertise. The knowledge of Ansuz additionally calls us to hook up with our very very own intuition and internal guidance. Cultivate self-reflection, meditation, or journaling practices to get right of entry to your very non-public inner know-how. Trust the insights that rise up from internal and integrate them with the out of doors expertise you acquire.

Share your knowledge: As you deepen your statistics and advantage insights, percent your know-how with others. Engage in significant conversations, mentor folks that are seeking out steering, or write and specific your thoughts through numerous mediums. By sharing your knowledge, you are making contributions to the collective boom and inspire others on their very very very own trips of looking for understanding.

The Ansuz rune invites us to embark on a lifelong adventure of on the lookout for records and growing our facts of the location. By actively enticing in the pursuit of knowledge, listening to smart endorse, and integrating statistics into our lives, we align ourselves with the transformative power of Ansuz. Embrace the know-how of others, consider your inner understanding, and percent your facts with the place. By doing so, you encompass the essence of the Ansuz rune and invite profound non-public growth and perception into your lifestyles.

Chapter 4: Kenaz The Intuition

In the amazing realm of Viking Astrology, the Kenaz rune illuminates the course of instinct and inner knowledge. Known because the Intuition Rune, Kenaz offers people the electricity to faucet into their innate focus and put it to apply as a guiding pressure in selection-making and hassle-fixing. It beckons us to encompass our intuitive powers and navigate the complexities of lifestyles with readability and belief. Let us embark on a adventure of discovery and find the sensible steps to harnessing the transformative nature of the Kenaz rune.

Practical Points:

Cultivate self-recognition: Begin via the use of cultivating self-interest, which serves as the foundation for honing your intuitive abilities. Pay interest to your mind, feelings, and physical sensations. Practice mindfulness and interact in self-reflection to advantage deeper perception into your inner world. By records your self on a profound diploma, you create space for intuitive know-how to emerge.

Trust your instincts: Embrace the electricity of trusting your instincts. When confronted with options or stressful situations, take a second to tune into your internal knowing. Notice any on the spot gut emotions or diffused nudges guiding you in a particular direction. Trust that your intuition is a dependable compass, presenting precious guidance.

Engage in intuition-improving practices: Engage in practices that support the development and enhancement of your instinct. Meditation, visualization, and breathwork can assist quiet the mind, permitting intuitive insights to floor. Journaling and dream evaluation are effective equipment for exploring the symbols and messages that upward thrust up from your unconscious mind.

Seek solitude and silence: Find moments of solitude and silence to create area for instinct to flourish. In the stillness, you could higher attune yourself to the subtle whispers of your intuition. Disconnect from outside distractions and permit your self to be completely present, beginning the door to deep intuitive connections.

Pay hobby to synchronicities: Synchronicities, considerable coincidences that bring messages, are often signposts from the universe. Pay interest to the synchronicities that occur in your lifestyles. These can show up as repeated numbers, encounters with unique animals, or sudden encounters with humans. Reflect on their importance and don't forget the messages they'll preserve.

Engage in innovative expression: Engaging in innovative sports activities sports collectively with artwork, tune, or writing nurtures your intuitive skills. Creativity opens the channels of idea and connects you to the glide of intuitive information. Allow yourself to find out and specific your innermost thoughts and feelings via revolutionary mediums.

Follow your passions: Your passions and interests can function gateways to intuitive insights. When you engage in sports activities that ignite your enthusiasm, you align yourself collectively with your real self. Trust that the belongings you are interested in preserve significance and that pursuing them will provide valuable intuitive guidance.

Practice discernment: While intuition is a powerful device, it's miles important to stability it with discernment. Discernment allows you to evaluate the statistics obtained thru your instinct and decide its validity. Engage in critical wondering, acquire additional information at the equal time as important, and looking for awesome views earlier than making choices based totally mostly on intuitive insights.

Learn from beyond memories: Reflect on beyond reviews when your instinct guided you, and take a look at the outcomes. Consider instances in which you neglected or omitted intuitive signals. By mastering from the ones reports, you can refine your capability to decide real intuitive guidance and believe it wholeheartedly.

Trust the timing: Intuitive insights often show themselves of their very personal time. Be affected individual and agree with the timing of the messages to procure. Avoid forcing intuitive answers or searching for them while they will be now not effortlessly to be had. Embrace the information of the Kenaz rune by means of using way of permitting intuitive steerage to spread honestly.

By embracing the strength of instinct and integrating it into your choice-making and trouble-solving methods, you align your self with the transformative energy of the Kenaz rune. Cultivate self-attention, receive as actual together along with your instincts, and interact in practices that decorate your intuitive abilities. Embrace solitude, pay attention to synchronicities, and nurture your progressive expression. Remember to balance your intuition with discernment and study from past memories. Trust the timing of intuitive insights, and allow them to guide you in your direction. By doing so, you honor the statistics of the Kenaz rune and navigate lifestyles's complexities with clarity, insight, and self belief.

Kenaz - The Intuition Rune

Within the hard tapestry of Viking astrology, the Kenaz rune shines as a beacon of intuitive focus. Like a flickering flame within the dark, it illuminates the direction to self-discovery and aids in selection-making. In this financial disaster, we can find out the profound powers bestowed thru the Kenaz rune and find out the manner to harness instinct as a guiding strain in navigating lifestyles's complicated alternatives.

Cultivating Awareness:

The Kenaz rune reminds us to domesticate a heightened sense of interest in our every day lives. To tap into its intuitive strength, exercising mindfulness and discover ways to check the diffused nuances of your environment. Slow down and interact all your senses. Notice the factors of hobby, sounds, smells, and textures of the area round you. By cultivating this cognizance, you open the door to receiving intuitive messages out of your environment.

Trusting Your Gut:

Intuition frequently manifests as a "intestine feeling" or an instinctive know-how that guides us in the proper direction. Learn to believe your intestine and honor those intuitive nudges that get up inside you. These inner promptings are the whispers of historical know-how, a connection to the deep nicely of facts internal your being. By being attentive to your instinct, you may make decisions with extra clarity and self assurance.

Dream Interpretation:

Dreams are a effective street through which instinct speaks to us. The Kenaz rune encourages us to be aware of our goals and find out their hidden meanings. Keep a dream mag with the aid of your bedside and record your desires upon waking. Reflect at the symbols, emotions, and messages inner your goals. Over time, patterns and insights might also moreover emerge, imparting guidance and deeper expertise.

Symbolic Language:

The Kenaz rune invites us to discover the language of symbols and signs. Symbols preserve outstanding importance in Norse mythology and Viking way of lifestyles. Pay interest to regular symbols in your life, every inside the physical and metaphysical geographical regions. They may additionally moreover seem in desires, nature, or perhaps within the ordinary gadgets and research you stumble upon. Trust your instinct to decipher the hidden messages conveyed through those symbols.

Creative Expression:

Creativity is in detail linked to instinct. The Kenaz rune encourages you to interact in innovative endeavors as a manner of tapping into your intuitive drift. Whether thru portray, writing, track, or a few exceptional shape of innovative expression, allow your instinct to manual your progressive method. Surrender to the waft of belief and permit your intuition guide the brushstrokes of your creativity.

Silence and Solitude:

Intuition flourishes in moments of silence and solitude. Create wallet of stillness for your day, loose from distractions and noise. Find a tranquil region in which you may be on my own together along with your mind and feelings. In this sacred area, your instinct can speak loudest. Use this time for introspection, meditation, or virtually to be present with yourself. Listen cautiously, and you can pay attention the whispers of your instinct.

Journaling and Reflection:

Writing may be a powerful device for unlocking intuition. Set apart regular time for journaling and self-reflected picture. Use this exercising to discover your mind, emotions, and opinions. Pose questions to your self and permit your intuition to manual your responses. Trust the spontaneous insights that arise as you pour your mind onto the web page.

Balancing Intuition with Rationality:

While intuition is a valuable manual, it is essential to strike a balance with rational wondering. The Kenaz rune encourages you to honor every your intuitive expertise and your logical thoughts. Seek to combine the two, permitting intuition to tell your selections on the same time as moreover thinking about practical problems. Embrace the wedding of intuition and purpose, developing a harmonious combination that enables your adventure.

Embrace the radiant power of the Kenaz rune, allowing its flame to light up the route of your intuition. Trust for your inner knowing, and let it guide you in the direction of a lifestyles complete of motive, readability, and real desire-making. As you preserve your adventure via the nation-states of Viking astrology, continue to be open to the mysteries that unfold, for they preserve the keys to unlocking the secrets and techniques and techniques of your proper self.

Gebo - The Rune of Balance

In the outstanding tapestry of Viking astrology, the Gebo rune weaves a thread of stability and harmony. It symbolizes the delicate dance among giving and receiving, the interaction of relationships, and the significance of making balanced lifestyles picks. In this bankruptcy, we can find out the profound information embodied thru the Gebo rune and find out practical ways to nurture relationships and domesticate equilibrium in our lives.

The Exchange of Gifts:

The Gebo rune reminds us of the electricity of reciprocity and the splendor of mutual exchange. Cultivate the spirit of giving and receiving for your relationships, no longer best in fabric phrases however also in emotional assist, records, and kindness. Be aware of the wishes and dreams of others, and offer your presence and assist in which it is wished. Similarly, permit your self to get maintain of the gadgets of others with gratitude and beauty.

Balanced Communication:

Effective verbal exchange is important for preserving harmonious relationships. The

Gebo rune encourages you to pay attention actively and speak in fact and respectfully. Strive for balanced talk wherein all activities have the opportunity to specific their thoughts and emotions. Practice empathy, looking for to understand others' perspectives earlier than responding. By fostering open and balanced conversation, you can build sturdy and harmonious connections.

Reciprocal Relationships:

Nurture your relationships with the useful resource of cultivating a feel of reciprocity. Recognize the importance of identical partnership and mutual help. Seek to create a balanced provide-and-take dynamic, wherein every parties make contributions to the increase and well-being of the relationship. Find methods to assist and uplift every other, celebrating successes and supplying solace in times of want.

Emotional Boundaries:

Maintaining healthful emotional boundaries is important for setting up balanced relationships. The Gebo rune encourages you to honor your very personal emotional nicely-being at the same time as respecting the bounds of others. Be aware of your very non-public desires and barriers, and speak them sincerely to others. Similarly, be receptive to the limits set via others, imparting records and assist with out overstepping.

Life Choices and Priorities:

The Gebo rune invites you to assess your existence options and priorities, making sure they align along with your values and produce stability on your ordinary well-being. Take time to reflect to your commitments and obligations. Are they in concord together with your non-public desires and dreams? Are you neglecting any vital factors of your life? Strive for a balanced approach, making aware alternatives that assist your holistic boom and happiness.

Self-Care and Self-Love:

Maintaining stability in relationships requires nurturing oneself. The Gebo rune reminds you to prioritize self-care and self-love. Make time for activities that refill your electricity and convey you pleasure. Set barriers to defend your bodily, highbrow, and emotional properly-being. Treat yourself with kindness and compassion, acknowledging your non-public nicely really worth and nurturing a wholesome relationship with your self.

Harmony with Nature:

Connecting with the natural international can assist repair balance on your existence. Spend time in nature, embracing its splendor and calmness. Engage in practices that deepen your connection to the natural rhythms of the Earth. Observe the cycles of the seasons, recognizing the ebb and go with the flow of life. By aligning your self with the harmonious power of nature, you can locate more stability internal.

Gratitude Practice:

Gratitude is a effective device for cultivating balance and harmony. The Gebo rune invitations you to include a everyday gratitude exercise. Take time each day to reflect at the advantages in your lifestyles, each big and small. Express gratitude to others for their presence, assist, and contributions. By cultivating a mindset of gratitude, you may shift your attention to the tremendous components of existence and foster a extra enjoy of stability and contentment.

Embrace the understanding of the Gebo rune, permitting it to guide you on a direction of balanced relationships and alternatives. Strive for reciprocity, each in your interactions with others and for your dating with yourself. Seek harmony in all components of your existence, spotting that stability is an ongoing journey, requiring popularity, mindfulness, and aware attempt. As you combine the lessons of the Gebo rune into your every day lifestyles, may additionally furthermore you discover success inside the symphony of balanced connections and alternatives that shape your specific destiny.

Chapter 5: Wunjo The Pleasure

Within the tapestry of Viking astrology, the Wunjo rune radiates with the essence of delight and contentment. It invites us to embody the easy pleasures in existence and are attempting to find happiness in regular studies. In this bankruptcy, we are able to embark on a journey to find out the profound know-how embodied via the Wunjo rune, exploring sensible techniques to infuse our lives with pleasure and cultivate a revel in of fulfillment.

Cultivating Gratitude:

Gratitude is a key pathway to unlocking the pride within. The Wunjo rune encourages us to domesticate a regular gratitude workout. Take time each day to reflect on the advantages and outstanding components of your lifestyles. Appreciate the people, opinions, and matters that convey you delight. By consciously that specialize in gratitude, you invite greater happiness into your life.

Embracing the Present Moment:

The Wunjo rune invitations us to definitely embody the prevailing 2d. Practice mindfulness, becoming aware about the sensations, mind, and emotions that stand up in every 2d. Engage in sports activities that convey you pleasure, whether or not or no longer it's far savoring a delicious meal, relishing the beauty of nature, or immersing your self in a innovative organisation. By really immersing yourself within the gift, you could experience the richness and satisfaction that existence has to offer.

Nurturing Relationships:

Meaningful connections with others make contributions to our ordinary experience of satisfaction and properly-being. The Wunjo rune encourages us to nurture our relationships and create areas for pleasure to flourish. Spend first-rate time with cherished ones, undertaking sports activities that carry you closer collectively. Share laughter, engage in heartfelt conversations, and specific your appreciation for one another. Cultivate an surroundings of affection, resource, and delight inner your relationships.

Pursuing Passions and Hobbies:

Engaging in sports that align with our passions and hobbies can deliver big pride into our lives. The Wunjo rune invites you to discover your passions and locate time for pursuits that ignite your spirit. Whether it's far playing a musical tool, painting, gardening, or every one-of-a-kind creative pursuit, immerse yourself in sports activities that supply you pleasure and success. Allow yourself the freedom to specific your real self through these endeavors.

Finding Joy in Nature:

The splendor and tranquility of nature have the electricity to uplift our spirits and evoke a enjoy of joy. The Wunjo rune encourages you to spend time in nature, connecting with its restoration strength. Take walks in natural surroundings, concentrate to the sounds of birdsong, or really sit in stillness, appreciating the beauty of the herbal global. Allow nature's serenity to nourish your soul and produce you a feel of deep pride.

Cultivating Mind-Body Balance:

The Wunjo rune reminds us of the importance of nurturing our bodily and intellectual nicely-being. Cultivate practices that sell stability and commonplace fitness. Engage in normal exercising, eat nourishing food, and get sufficient relaxation. Explore mindfulness practices, along with meditation or yoga, to domesticate a enjoy of internal calm and delight. By searching after your thoughts and body, you can experience more ranges of happiness and nicely-being.

Spreading Joy:

The satisfaction we domesticate internal ourselves has the power to radiate outward and really impact those spherical us. The Wunjo rune encourages acts of kindness and compassion. Find procedures to spread pride to others, whether or not or no longer or not thru a smile, a type word, or a small act of generosity. Celebrate the accomplishments and successes of others, helping them of their pursuit of happiness. By sharing joy, we create a ripple effect of positivity within the international.

Embracing Simplicity:

In a global regularly complete of complexity, the Wunjo rune reminds us of the splendor and pleasure observed in simplicity. Take time to recognise the small pleasures of existence, together with the warm temperature of daylight, the flavor of a delicious meal, or the laughter of loved ones. Simplify your existence through manner of manner of decluttering your bodily area and freeing attachments to fabric possessions. Embrace a minimalist attitude, specializing in what truely brings you pleasure.

As you embark on a journey to encompass the expertise of the Wunjo rune, might also additionally you discover pride within the normal moments and cultivate a deep experience of contentment. Open yourself to the huge pride that surrounds you and allow it to permeate your being. Embrace the simplicity, gratitude, and connections that deliver you happiness, developing a existence complete of satisfaction and fulfillment.

Hagalaz - The Rune of Catastrophe

The Hagalaz rune, often misunderstood as a picture of chaos and destruction, holds a deeper due to this in the geographical areas of Viking astrology. In this financial ruin, we're capable of dispel the misconceptions surrounding the Hagalaz rune and find its real essence as a catalyst for boom and rebuilding in the face of difficult instances.

We will find out realistic strategies to recognize the possibilities for transformation that upward thrust up from moments of upheaval and embody the know-how in the Hagalaz rune.

Embracing Change:

The Hagalaz rune serves as a reminder that exchange is an inherent a part of existence's journey. Rather than resisting or fearing trade, embody it as an possibility for increase and transformation. Understand that now and again, upheaval is crucial to pave the way for extremely-modern-day beginnings. Cultivate a mind-set of adaptability and flexibility, permitting yourself to waft with the currents of exchange rather than preventing in competition to them.

Recognizing Patterns:

The Hagalaz rune encourages you to be privy to normal patterns or cycles to your life. Patterns may be diffused or greater said, however they frequently supply essential messages and instructions. Take time to reflect at the conditions, relationships, or studies that appear to duplicate. Are there underlying patterns or issues? By spotting those styles, you gain notion into regions that could require hobby or transformation.

Facing Challenges:

Challenges and setbacks are an inevitable part of life. The Hagalaz rune teaches us not to pull away from those moments of adversity however to stand them with courage and resilience. Rather than viewing challenges as barriers, see them as opportunities for boom and self-discovery. Embrace the commands they offer and accept as true with that they will in the end bring about a more potent, wiser model of your self.

Embracing the Shadow:

Within the place of the Hagalaz rune lies an invitation to embrace and combine our shadow factors—the factors of ourselves that we regularly avoid or reject. Explore the factors of yourself that you can endure in mind "dark" or uncomfortable. By acknowledging and accepting the ones elements, you can combine them into your being, fostering wholeness and self-beauty. Embracing the shadow permits for personal boom and a deeper know-how of oneself.

Rebuilding and Renewal:

Just because the storm passes and clears the route for modern increase, the Hagalaz rune represents the opportunity for rebuilding and renewal after difficult situations. When confronted with upheaval, allow yourself the time and location to heal and acquire your energy. Embrace the transformative power inside you and focus on rebuilding your existence with cause and reason. Trust that new possibilities and possibilities will rise up from the ashes of the past.

Self-Reflection and Learning:

The Hagalaz rune invites you to engage in self-mirrored picture in some unspecified time inside the destiny of instances of hassle. Take time to contemplate the education and insights that get up from difficult evaluations. What are you able to test from them? How are you able to boom from the expertise received? Through introspection, you could navigate the route of transformation with greater consciousness and goal.

Seeking Support:

During times of upheaval, searching for guide from depended on humans can provide solace and steerage. Reach out to buddies, circle of relatives, or experts who can provide a listening ear, recommendation, or assets. Surround yourself with a supportive community this is conscious and empathizes together with your adventure. Remember, you do not want to stand demanding situations on my own, and looking for manual is an indication of strength.

Cultivating Resilience:

The Hagalaz rune requires the cultivation of resilience—the functionality to get better from adversity and locate power within the face of demanding situations. Embrace practices that nourish your resilience, together with self-care, mindfulness, and healthful coping mechanisms. Cultivate an internal electricity that lets in you to conform and increase, even inside the midst of troubles.

As you navigate the terrain of the Hagalaz rune, don't forget that it is thru moments of upheaval that we frequently enjoy the maximum profound increase and transformation. Embrace the understanding in the rune, spotting that annoying conditions are possibilities for renewal and rebuilding. Trust for your internal power, and keep in mind that you very own the resilience and focus critical to triumph over any obstacle for your path.

Chapter 6: Nauthiz The Alertness

In the area of Viking astrology, the Nauthiz rune holds a essential significance as the symbol of alertness and preparedness. In this financial ruin, we will discover the deep records and practical applications of the Nauthiz rune in navigating lifestyles's annoying situations. By expertise the importance of vigilance and growing resilience in the face of adversity, we will harness the power of the Nauthiz rune to adapt and thrive. Let us delve into the profound teachings of the Nauthiz rune and discover how it is able to guide us on our path.

Recognizing the Need for Vigilance:

The Nauthiz rune reminds us to be alert and aware about the occasions and events unfolding round us. Stay attuned to every the inner and outdoor indicators that may suggest capability annoying conditions or possibilities. Cultivate mindfulness and self-reputation to understand the diffused shifts in strength and make informed selections.

Developing Resilience:

Resilience is the functionality to get higher and adapt within the face of adversity. The Nauthiz rune encourages us to assemble inner energy and fortitude to withstand existence's challenges. Practice self-care and domesticate emotional properly-being to nurture resilience. Remember that setbacks aren't screw ups but opportunities for growth and transformation.

Seeking Inner Resources:

In instances of problem, turn inward to get proper of entry in your inner property and strengths. The Nauthiz rune teaches us to take into account in our talents and faucet into our knowledge and enjoy to navigate tough situations. Connect at the side of your intuition and draw upon your internal reserves of braveness and determination. Reflect on beyond accomplishments and demanding situations conquer, acknowledging your internal strength and resilience.

Embracing Preparedness:

The Nauthiz rune reminds us of the importance of preparedness. While we can't are anticipating each venture which could upward thrust up, we will expand a mind-set of preparedness and take proactive steps to mitigate dangers. This might also moreover comprise acquiring new competencies, building aid networks, or maintaining emergency belongings. By getting geared up for functionality barriers, we beautify our potential to respond correctly.

Cultivating Adaptability:

The Nauthiz rune requires adaptability in the face of surprising situations. Life is continuously converting, and the functionality to regulate and adapt is important for personal growth. Embrace the unknown with hobby and openness, permitting yourself to discover new views and possibilities. Be willing to permit cross of rigid expectancies and discover current answers at the same time as faced with demanding situations.

Learning from Adversity:

Adversity may be a profound trainer, offering valuable commands and insights. The Nauthiz rune invitations us to view challenges as possibilities for boom and self-discovery. When confronted with adversity, take time for reflected picture and introspection. Ask your self what schooling may be positioned out and the way you may emerge more potent from the experience. Embrace the notice obtained from navigating difficult times.

Building Support Networks:

The Nauthiz rune emphasizes the importance of constructing sturdy beneficial aid networks. Seek out relationships and connections with those who offer encouragement, steerage, and records. Surround your self with a network that uplifts and helps you throughout tough instances. Likewise, offer your guide and lend a assisting hand to others in want.

Developing Problem-Solving Skills:

The Nauthiz rune encourages the improvement of hassle-fixing abilties. Cultivate a proactive thoughts-set with the aid of breaking stressful situations into practicable obligations. Practice crucial wondering and creative hassle-fixing techniques. Explore taken into consideration considered one of a type procedures and views even as coping with barriers. Develop your capability to adapt and locate present day answers.

By embracing the schooling of the Nauthiz rune, we cultivate alertness, resilience, and adaptability within the face of adversity. Recognize the importance of vigilance and preparedness, drawing upon internal resources and searching out guide whilst wished. Embrace challenges as opportunities for increase and getting to know, and boom problem-fixing skills to navigate lifestyles's barriers. Remember, via embodying the attention of the Nauthiz rune, you may upward thrust above adversity and forge your course with braveness and strength.

Isa - The Rune of Patience

In the area of Viking astrology, the Isa rune holds the profound expertise of staying strength and organized. This economic break will find out the importance of the Isa rune, its teachings on the price of timing and perseverance, and the way we're capable of encompass those trends in our lives. By records and embodying the essence of Isa, we will navigate stressful situations, make wiser picks, and cultivate a feel of internal calm. Let us embark on a journey of exploration into the depths of the Isa rune and find out its transformative strength.

Embracing the Wisdom of Timing:

The Isa rune teaches us the importance of timing in our lives. It reminds us that the whole thing has its season, and a few matters cannot be rushed. Embrace the natural drift of sports and consider inside the unfolding of time. Practice endurance and allow situations to broaden in their private rhythm. By aligning ourselves with the proper timing, we can make higher picks and achieve more favorable results.

Cultivating Inner Stillness:

Isa invitations us to domesticate inner stillness amidst the busyness of existence. In moments of uncertainty or impatience, take a pause and hook up with your inner self. Practice meditation or mindfulness strategies to quiet the mind and find out solace inside the present 2nd. Embrace the calmness that contains persistence and permit it guide your movements.

Nurturing Perseverance:

Perseverance is a key extremely good related to the Isa rune. It encourages us to stay committed and dedicated to our desires, despite the fact that faced with challenges or setbacks. Embrace the prolonged-term view and recognize that fulfillment frequently calls for time and effort. Develop resilience and preserve moving ahead, know-how that each step brings you toward your selected final results.

Embodying Grace beneath Pressure:

In moments of strain or strain, the Isa rune teaches us to stay composed and level-headed. Rather than succumbing to impatience or frustration, encompass grace and keep your internal equilibrium. Practice deep respiration strategies or engage in sports activities that sell rest and stress consolation. By cultivating grace under stress, you can navigate demanding situations with readability and know-how.

Trusting the Process:

The Isa rune reminds us to bear in mind in the method of existence. It teaches us that there may be focus in ready and that no longer the whole thing may be rushed or forced. Trust that the universe has its private timing, and that the whole thing unfolds as it need to. Release the want for instant results and trust that the proper possibilities will show up whilst the time is right.

Seeking Inner Guidance:

Patience opens the door to inner steering and intuition. The Isa rune encourages us to listen to our internal voice and believe our instincts. Take time for introspection and reflected picture, permitting your internal knowledge to guide your choices. Develop a deeper connection with your instinct via the usage of way of schooling active listening and honoring your internal know-how.

Embracing the Beauty of Silence:

Silence is a effective tool within the realm of staying strength. The Isa rune invitations us to recognize the splendor of silence and recognize its transformative capability. Take moments of silence and solitude to recharge and find out clarity. Disconnect from outside distractions and immerse yourself in the stillness internal. Embrace the attention that emerges from those moments of silence.

Applying Patience in Daily Life:

Practical application of staying strength in our each day lives may have a profound effect. Practice staying power on your interactions with others, permitting them the distance and time they want. Embrace staying strength on your pastimes and endeavors, knowledge that development takes time. Nurture staying energy for your private increase journey, information that transformation unfolds grade by grade.

By embracing the lessons of the Isa rune, we domesticate patience, perseverance, and consider inside the timing of lifestyles. Embrace the notice of timing, domesticate internal stillness, and nurture perseverance. Trust the technique, are seeking for inner steering, and appreciate the beauty of silence. Apply staying energy on your every day existence and witness its transformative strength. Remember, through embodying the essence of Isa, you can navigate existence's demanding situations with awareness, grace, and inner electricity.

Chapter 7: The Harvest

In the arena of Viking astrology, the Jera rune represents the cycles of life, the seasons of boom, and the bountiful harvest. This financial ruin will find out the profound significance of the Jera rune, its connection to sowing and reaping, and the way we are able to harness its energy for non-public growth and fulfillment. By information and aligning ourselves with the energies of Jera, we are able to domesticate wonderful actions, intentions, and a revel in of abundance in our lives. Let us embark on a adventure of exploration into the depths of the Jera rune and find out its transformative energy.

Embracing the Natural Cycles:

The Jera rune reminds us of the natural cycles of existence, symbolized via the converting seasons. Just as nature memories cycles of boom, fruition, and rot, so can we. Embrace the understanding that each segment has its purpose and that each revel in contributes to your personal increase and improvement. By aligning ourselves with the ones natural cycles, we're capable of locate concord and go with the flow in our lives.

Sowing the Seeds of Intentions:

The Jera rune teaches us the importance of sowing the seeds of powerful intentions. Just as a farmer carefully selects and sows seeds for a bountiful harvest, we can also consciously plant the seeds of our goals, desires, and desires. Take time to mirror on what you desire to cultivate on your lifestyles. Set smooth intentions and take stimulated actions within the course in their consciousness. Trust that your efforts will undergo fruit in due time.

Nurturing Growth and Development:

To enjoy a fruitful harvest, we need to nurture the increase and development of what we've got sown. The Jera rune encourages us to take ordinary and aware motion inside the route of our dreams. Cultivate staying power and perseverance as you have a tendency to the seeds you've got were given planted. Embrace a growth mind-set, continuously reading, adapting, and increasing your know-how and abilities.

Recognizing the Importance of Patience:

Patience is a key extraordinary associated with the Jera rune. It reminds us that increase and transformation take time. Embrace the technique, despite the fact that outcomes might not be right away. Trust that every step you are taking is contributing to the overall harvest. Cultivate staying strength for your every day lifestyles, on your interactions with others, and in your very private non-public journey of boom.

Honoring the Harvest:

The Jera rune invitations us to honor and feature a laugh the harvest in our lives. Take time to renowned and understand the culmination of your exertions. Reflect to your accomplishments, both large and small. Express gratitude for the abundance that surrounds you. Share your advantages with others, understanding that the act of giving and sharing amplifies the delight of the harvest.

Embracing the Lessons of Failure:

Just due to the fact the Jera rune represents the bountiful harvest, it additionally reminds us of the education that come from setbacks and disasters. Embrace the understanding obtained from past research, even those which could have regarded like disasters on the time. Recognize that those education make a contribution for your private boom and shape your destiny harvests. Embrace a increase attitude that perspectives demanding situations as opportunities for reading and development.

Cultivating a Mindset of Abundance:

The Jera rune teaches us to domesticate a mind-set of abundance. Let bypass of shortage thinking and embody the belief that there may be enough for genuinely all people. Trust in the universe's abundance and realize that you are deserving of the benefits that come your way. Practice gratitude for the abundance that exists in your existence, and you may attraction to more abundance in go returned.

Connecting with Nature's Rhythms:

Nature gives a powerful instance of the cycles and rhythms embodied through the Jera rune. Spend time in nature, looking at and connecting with its seasonal adjustments. Align your sports sports and intentions with the herbal rhythms of the Earth. Incorporate nature-based totally practices into your lifestyles, inclusive of gardening, woodland bathing, or definitely walking in herbal environment. Allow nature to encourage and manual you in your journey of growth and harvest.

By embracing the classes of the Jera rune, we domesticate an expertise of life's cycles, sow the seeds of excellent intentions, and nurture our private boom and development. We honor the harvest, include the instructions of failure, and domesticate a mindset of abundance. We connect with nature's rhythms and discover harmony inside ourselves and in our interactions with the world. Remember, through aligning yourself with the energies of Jera, you may harness the electricity of first rate movements, intentions, and a bountiful harvest in your very own existence.

Eihwaz - The Creative and Protective Rune

In the location of Viking astrology, the Eihwaz rune holds profound significance as a picture of both creativity and protection. This financial smash will delve into the depths of the Eihwaz rune, exploring its transformative energy and the manner it may be harnessed to triumph over barriers and cultivate resilience. Through the exploration of Eihwaz, we are able to discover the relationship between imagination, internal power, and the capability to navigate the disturbing situations of lifestyles. Let us embark on a journey of know-how and faucet into the transformative electricity of the Eihwaz rune.

Embracing the Power of Imagination:

The Eihwaz rune invitations us to tap into our creativeness and progressive capability. It encourages us to assume beyond conventional boundaries and find out new possibilities. By embracing our innovative nature, we are able to discover present day solutions to annoying conditions, enlarge our views, and open doors to new opportunities. Allow your imagination to guide you, unleash your creativity, and method troubles with a glowing and imaginitive mind-set.

Nurturing Resilience and Inner Strength:

Just because the Eihwaz rune represents the powerful yew tree, recognized for its electricity and resilience, it reminds us of the significance of nurturing our very private inner strength. Cultivate resilience via developing a effective thoughts-set, cultivating self-notion, and embracing demanding situations as possibilities for boom. Draw upon the electricity of the Eihwaz rune to stay steadfast inside the face of adversity, understanding that interior you lies the electricity to go through and triumph over.

Overcoming Obstacles:

The Eihwaz rune teaches us that barriers are not roadblocks but stepping stones on our journey. Embrace the commands and boom possibilities that annoying situations present. Shift your mind-set from viewing limitations as burdens to perceiving them as catalysts for non-public improvement. Tap into the protective electricity of Eihwaz to navigate through difficult situations with grace and backbone.

Seeking Guidance and Protection:

The Eihwaz rune serves as a guiding strain and defensive picture. Just due to the fact the yew tree shields and permits lifestyles, Eihwaz offers a feel of safety and steerage. Trust your intuition and are searching for internal guidance even as faced with tough alternatives. Meditate on the Eihwaz rune to hook up with its defensive electricity, locating solace inside the information which you are supported and guided in your route.

Honoring Endings and New Beginnings:

The Eihwaz rune represents the cyclical nature of life, symbolizing the transition from endings to new beginnings. Embrace the facts of Eihwaz through spotting that each completing brings forth new opportunities and growth. Release attachments to the beyond, consist of alternate, and welcome the functionality that awaits. By honoring the natural cycles of existence, you may go along with the drift with the transformative power of Eihwaz and embody the ever-evolving nature of your journey.

Cultivating Inner Balance:

The Eihwaz rune teaches us the significance of preserving internal balance. Balance your bodily, emotional, and spiritual nicely-being to cultivate resilience and navigate thru lifestyles's stressful situations. Practice self-care, interact in sports that convey you pride, and connect to nature. The balance you create inside your self will offer a strong basis from which to overcome barriers and display up your innovative functionality.

Embracing the Unknown:

Just because the Eihwaz rune represents the unexplored depths of the wooded vicinity, it encourages us to encompass the unknown and challenge into uncharted territories. Release the worry of the sudden and step outdoor your comfort place. Embrace the unknown with interest and an open mind, knowledge that in the depths of uncertainty lie opportunities for boom, discovery, and transformation.

Harnessing the Power of Endurance:

Endurance is a key splendid associated with the Eihwaz rune. It reminds us to live devoted to our goals, even if confronted with challenges or setbacks. Embrace the lengthy-term view, information that lasting achievements often require staying power and perseverance. Draw energy from the Eihwaz rune and stay steadfast in your route, expertise that with determination and resilience, you could overcome any obstacle.

By exploring the transformative power of the Eihwaz rune, we faucet into our revolutionary capability, domesticate internal energy, and navigate demanding situations with resilience and imagination.

Embrace the energy of your creativeness, nurture your inner strength, and triumph over barriers with grace and determination. Seek steerage and protection from the Eihwaz rune, honoring endings and new beginnings as you domesticate internal stability. Embrace the unknown, harness the electricity of persistence, and unencumber the transformative potential that lies interior you. Remember, the Eihwaz rune serves as a reminder that creativity and protection bypass hand in hand, imparting a supply of notion and resilience in your adventure through existence.

Chapter 8: The Rune Of Protection

In the world of Viking astrology, the Algiz rune stands as a effective image of safety and steering. This bankruptcy will find out the deep-rooted importance of Algiz, losing mild on its characteristic in imparting protection and finding solace amidst lifestyles's uncertainties. By understanding the protecting abilties of the Algiz rune, we are able to discover ways to navigate tough situations with more self guarantee and are searching for guidance from higher resources. Let us embark on a adventure of discovery and tap into the protecting energy of Algiz.

Connecting with the Divine:

The Algiz rune serves as a gateway to hook up with the divine forces that watch over us. It symbolizes the sacred connection among humanity and the spiritual geographical areas. Embrace the opportunity to boom a deep experience of spirituality and are in search of steerage from better resources.

Cultivate practices which include meditation, prayer, or communing with nature to foster this connection and locate solace in the presence of divine protection.

Seeking Guidance in Times of Uncertainty:

Life frequently gives us with uncertain and difficult situations. During such instances, the Algiz rune encourages us to are trying to find steerage and protection. Tap into your intuition and inner records to make informed alternatives. Trust your instincts and are in search of recommendation from relied on belongings who can provide clarity and steering. Embracing the protecting power of Algiz lets in us to navigate the complexities of lifestyles with greater self guarantee and reality.

Establishing Boundaries and Protection:

Just because of the truth the Algiz rune represents the antlers of the elk, it symbolizes the popularity quo of limitations and safety. Embrace the power to set up healthful boundaries for your existence. Protect your physical, emotional, and non secular properly-being with the aid of putting limits on what's suitable to you. Draw upon the strength of Algiz to guard your self from horrific affects and guard your non-public region.

Cultivating Inner Strength and Resilience:

The Algiz rune reminds us of the inner power and resilience we private. Embrace disturbing conditions as opportunities for boom and improvement. Cultivate a robust sense of self and a notion for your capabilities. Embody the protective electricity of Algiz to conquer limitations and setbacks, knowledge that you personal the inner strength to persevere and thrive.

Finding Safety and Sanctuary:

The Algiz rune serves as a picture of safety and sanctuary. Create a sacred location to your life wherein you could retreat, recharge, and discover solace. It can be a bodily space internal your home or a highbrow location you create thru meditation or visualization. Utilize this location to are searching for secure haven on the identical time as you experience overwhelmed or in need of safety. The power of Algiz will envelop you, offering a enjoy of protection and luxury.

Embracing Intuition and Instincts:

The Algiz rune encourages us to include our intuition and instincts as valuable gear for safety and steerage. Trust the inner voice that speaks to you and pay attention to the diffused messages of your instincts. Allow your intuition to guide your actions and alternatives, primary you in the route of the direction of safety and safety. Embody the electricity of Algiz and consist of the statistics that lies interior.

Honoring the Cycle of Life:

Just because the Algiz rune represents the interconnectedness of all life, it reminds us to honor the cycle of lifestyles and our region internal it. Embrace the information that the entirety is attached, and each revel in serves a purpose. Trust that the protective power of Algiz will manual you via the us of americaand downs of existence, assisting you on your journey.

Gratitude for Protection:

Express gratitude for the protecting power of Algiz to your lifestyles. Take a 2d every day to famend the protection you receive and the steering you're attempting to find. Cultivate a experience of appreciation for the tactics wherein Algiz shields you from harm and gives a experience of protection. By expressing gratitude, you invite extra protective energy into your lifestyles.

By exploring the protecting developments of the Algiz rune, we are able to cultivate a deeper feel of security and steerage. Connect with the divine, are searching out steerage in unsure instances, and set up healthful obstacles. Cultivate internal energy and resilience, locating protection and sanctuary internal your existence. Embrace your intuition and instincts, honoring the cycle of existence. Express gratitude for the protecting strength of Algiz, know-how that you are supported and guided to your journey. Embody the protecting energy of Algiz and flow beforehand with confidence, knowing which you are shielded through its effective presence.

Sowilo - The Balance of Stress and Health

In the arena of Viking astrology, the Sowilo rune shines as a image of slight and strength. This bankruptcy delves into the relationship among stress, bodily fitness, and the Sowilo rune, providing insights and practical strategies to encompass a balanced method to life's stressful conditions for normal well-being. By information the have an impact on of the Sowilo rune, we're capable of harness its electricity to optimize our physical fitness and manage stress correctly. Let us find out the harmonious stability among stress and health via the knowledge of Sowilo.

Embracing Inner Radiance:

The Sowilo rune represents the radiant strength of the sun and the internal moderate inner every mother and father. Embrace your internal radiance and understand that self-care is critical for present day well-being. Cultivate practices that nourish your spirit, inclusive of meditation, yoga, or spending time in nature. By embracing your internal slight, you'll radiate positivity and resilience, which can be critical for handling pressure and keeping top fitness.

Balancing Work and Rest:

The Sowilo rune reminds us of the significance of balancing artwork and rest in our lives. In our rapid-paced global, it's miles important to discover a wholesome equilibrium amongst productivity and self-care. Prioritize your well-being with the resource of putting boundaries and putting in a balance among art work, personal life, and entertainment. Take breaks, interact in sports that bring you pleasure, and make sure you get ok relaxation to recharge your power.

Nurturing Physical Health:

The Sowilo rune encourages us to prioritize our physical health. Engage in normal exercise or physical sports activities that deliver you satisfaction and help you preserve health. Explore numerous varieties of motion, which include strolling, dancing, or education martial arts, to discover what resonates with you. Nourish your frame with healthy, nutritious meals, and live hydrated to assist your everyday nicely-being.

Mindful Stress Management:

Stress is an inevitable part of lifestyles, however how we control it greatly influences our health. The Sowilo rune teaches us to embody a aware technique to strain manipulate. Practice mindfulness techniques together with deep respiratory, meditation, or journaling to center your self all through traumatic situations. Engage in sports that convey you calm and relaxation, such as taking a warm temperature bath or playing a interest. By cultivating mindfulness, you could navigate stress with greater readability and resilience.

Seeking Support:

In instances of stress, seeking out resource is essential for retaining balance and nicely-being. Reach out to relied on friends, own family individuals, or professionals who can offer steerage and assist. Share your issues and are searching out their attitude or recommendation. Remember that soliciting for assistance is a signal of electricity, and having a supportive network can significantly alleviate strain and beautify your normal health.

Embracing Positivity and Optimism:

The Sowilo rune reminds us to consist of positivity and optimism as gadget for managing strain and fostering accurate fitness. Cultivate a fine thoughts-set via schooling gratitude and that specialize within the awesome factors of your existence. Surround your self with powerful impacts, together with uplifting literature, music, or supportive groups. By embracing a effective outlook, you invite extra resilience and well-being into your existence.

Harmonizing Work-Life Balance:

Achieving paintings-life balance is a non-prevent adventure that calls for conscious effort. The Sowilo rune encourages us to reflect on our priorities and make aware alternatives that honor our well-being. Set practical desires and set up a time table that permits for each paintings and entertainment. Create boundaries among art work and personal existence to ensure dedicated time for self-care, rest, and rejuvenation.

Honoring Personal Boundaries:

Establishing and honoring personal limitations is vital for managing pressure and maintaining ideal fitness. Recognize your limits and communicate them assertively. Say "no" whilst crucial and prioritize your well-being. By honoring your barriers, you create area for self-care and decrease the threat of burnout.

By exploring the relationship amongst stress, bodily health, and the Sowilo rune, we are able to consist of a balanced technique to existence's demanding situations. Embrace your internal radiance, find out concord among art work and relaxation, and prioritize physical fitness. Practice aware stress manipulate, are in search of for assist whilst desired, and cultivate positivity and optimism. Harmonize art work-life balance, honor non-public obstacles, and navigate stress with resilience and properly-being. Embody the understanding of the Sowilo rune and permit its radiant energy to guide you on the path of balanced residing.

Chapter 9: Wolves Of The Sea

Who Were the Vikings?

The Vikings had been a tough and rapid of Nordic seafarers who spoke the Old Norse language and hailed from three international locations of Scandinavia: Denmark, Norway, and Sweden. The word 'Viking' in Old Norse without a doubt manner 'pirate raid'; warriors who went raiding in ships were described as 'going Viking.'

In European information, the Viking Age spanned greater or less from AD seven-hundred to 1100. The Viking Age end up a duration in which the Nordic peoples enjoyed a substantial military, financial, mercantile and population increase. Enabled via manner in their advanced seafaring skills and longships, many Vikings were able to leave Scandinavia and sail as an extended manner as Britain and Ireland and distinctive components of Europe. The presence of Viking interest at times has additionally been extended into the Mediterranean, North Africa the Middle East and Central Asia. And the Vikings did extra than surely discover: they conquered and mounted settlements, communities, and rules in various areas of northwestern Europe, European Russia, the North Atlantic islands and whilst far because the north-eastern coast of North America.

The spread of the Vikings and wider dissemination of Norse tradition additionally triggered strong foreign cultural influences into Scandinavia as properly, with profound historical tendencies going into later medieval periods.

Popular current conceptions of the Vikings frequently variety strongly from the real, complex way of life unearthed through archaeological findings and superb ancient sources. Vikings were alternately romanticized as noble savages, bloodthirsty piratical raiders, and intrepid adventurers. To in reality respect the profound impact that Viking manner of lifestyles and their legacy have left at the improvement of medieval Europe, we must appearance beyond the contemporary day cultural clichés and stereotypes, and get the real facts inside the lower returned of the wealthy, complicated and complicated way of life of the historic Norsemen.

Why Did The Vikings Raid?

Among the peoples of the technology, the Vikings of Scandinavia definitely weren't the handiest manner of existence to raid and pillage their pals. But Vikings virtually did raid greater frequently, and their raids have been by means of the use of far extra brutal and brutally green than the raids executed with the aid of different cultures. Many fear and grief- statistics exist that describe harrowing scenes of Viking longboats storming in from the waves, releasing hordes of bloodthirsty warriors that annihilated nearby defenders, laid waste to settlements and plundered strongholds and monasteries of their treasures. While historians have evolved severa competing theories through the years, no single reason need to very well supply an reason in the back of why the Vikings pillaged and made war with their buddies so frequently. Instead, modern-day-day-day historians look to a combination of different factors to help supply an cause at the back of the Viking's disposition for bloodshed.

One of the an lousy lot less well-known records about Scandinavian cultures is that, as a humans, the ancient Vikings existed for numerous hundred years in advance than they earned their reputation as plunderers. Until then, and for generations later, the Vikings were farmers, hunters, fishermen, gatherers and animal tenders. What also can need to have took place to shift their practices so dramatically from a mainly agrarian society to a warrior tradition? Many Viking historians receive as actual with it changed into the pressures in their burgeoning populace. Advances in agricultural strategies and the climate allowed the Scandinavians to develop extra meals and farm more land. An progressed surplus of food brought about a extra healthful populace, an extended lifestyles expectancy and, everyday, a everyday populace growth. Population pressures can also additionally have caused squabbles amongst neighboring clans, but it furthermore likely led a few Vikings to go away home, to discover and overcome new lands.

One of the pressures of a populace increase changed into a loss of region. The Scandinavians lived on islands or rugged peninsulas with little or no room to boom. Much of the terrain have become terrible for farming or truly too mountainous to inhabit, and for a good deal of the year, the climate turn out to be a tremendous deal less than hospitably bloodless. So Viking explorers may moreover have felt the want to find out a few special region, for cutting-edge beaches to settle and triumph over, or genuinely to take sources they lacked at home.

Another commonplace precept at the back of Viking expansionism grow to be that, at some point of their time, Charlemagne "used pressure and terror to Christianize all pagans," fundamental to competitive campaigns that provided many pagan tribes and clans the selection of baptism, conversion, or execution. As a give up give up result, Vikings and specific pagans in Europe resisted and preferred revenge. Indeed, whilst Christianity eventually did advantage a foothold in Scandinavia, it induced a critical conflict that fragmented Norway for nearly a century. At the identical time, England changed into affected by inner divisions; paired with the reality that plenty of Britain's settlements had been built alongside the coast or near navigable rivers, and for the purpose that many fiefdoms had been unwilling to offer useful resource to neighboring settlements allied to lordships they were feuding with, Viking ships basically had carte blanche as to whether or no longer to trade or raid due to the fact the possibilities supplied themselves.

Other historians be given as real with that some Viking raids may additionally have been completed by means of manner of exiles. The Vikings had properly-described laws that they used to control themselves. And one of the maximum not unusual punishments for convicted criminals have turn out to be exile: really, while criminals were sent off in a longboat with just a few substances and cautioned they will never pass back domestic, many could have taken to pillaging and plundering neighboring coastal settlements to live on.

Simple greed may also additionally additionally had been one of the motivators for Viking raids. Greed is a clean hassle: the

Vikings desired things that their buddies had -- coins, farm animals, spices, slaves, treasures, works of artwork, raw materials they could not acquire at home. They won't have favored those devices more than a few other way of life, and frequently they acquired these things through easy alternate and worldwide relations. But even as your humans have grown so skillful at crusing and preventing, why no longer certainly take some issue you favored? And the Vikings did this with the useful resource of the usage of raiding and pillaging. Greed can also additionally have completed a function in one of the greater infamous Viking raids passed off in 793. The Vikings struck and plundered Christian monastery at Lindisfarne in Northumbria; to masses of the rest of Britain, the form of directed attack on a Christian holy website online changed into galling, to say the least. However, unlike the rest of Britain, the Vikings were pagans, this means that they probably had little reservations approximately robbing a Christian church. To the Vikings, Christian monasteries made clean and tempting dreams: church buildings frequently stored precious treasures, which incorporates jewels, gold, books, loads of food and drink, and regularly cattle. Moreover, the monks inhabiting those locations have been frequently unarmed and will do little to protect themselves.

Eventually, it changed into believed that raiding have end up every bit part of Viking manner of life. Raiding may additionally additionally have started out a simple 'smash and seize' affair -- but over the years, some Vikings grew so exceptional at it that they have emerge as professional raiders, adopting the damaging act of pillaging and plundering as their foremost manner of incomes a livelihood. Over time, raiding and battle grew right right into a culture that fed on itself, until every male Scandinavian noticed it as a way to garner private wealth and increase their individual popularity through distinguishing themselves at the battlefield. War have emerge as such an indelible part of their way of life that more youthful Viking men were anticipated to check themselves in war, and it grow to be believed that death heroically on the battlefield changed into the only manner to ascend into the hallowed feasting corridor of the gods, Valhalla.

Chapter 10: The Rune Stones

The Norse inside the Viking Age may additionally need to, in fact, write and study using their very very very own non-standardized shape of the alphabet, referred to as runor, from in which we derive the modern-day phrase rune, this alphabet changed into carved on massively raised stones, often observed with complex, flowing illustrations of wolves, warriors, horses, and extra fantastical beasts. Runestones had been commonly brightly coloured – however, because of their exposure to the elements, no trace of those colorings stays to these days. And the Norsemen had been prolific writers: to at the prevailing time; there survives approximately three,000 runestones and over 6,000 runic inscriptions in Scandinavia. Runestones moreover served to mark the a long manner flung locations where the Norsemen went, and dozens of runestones can be located on the Isle of Man within the west, the Black Sea inside the east, Jamtland inside the north, and Schleswig within the south.

Runestones were commonly raised to glorify the dead, even though many also boast of first-rate deeds, including the development of crucial houses and monuments, to mark critical social and financial achievements, and to commemorate different important occasions. The giant majority of runestones, but, have been raised in memory of the useless. The maximum well-known runestones tell high-quality memories of those Vikings who perished on voyages to distant places lands, but the large majority have become committed to guys who died at domestic.

Yet, at least some runestones inform us a awesome deal more than the lives and deaths of well-known Vikings. Their powerful, poignant prose and dramatic illustrations screen a good deal approximately historical Norse mythology and faith. For example, the Altuna

Runestone in Uppland, an notable effigy formed from a block of strong granite, depicts Thor's brave voyage to capture the Midgard Serpent. With heroic prose and complex illustrations, the runestone tells of techniques Thor managed to snare the serpent with a fishing hook baited with the top of an ox. When the Serpent bit down at the ox-head, the hook caught at the roof of its mouth, startling it so violently that it shook Thor's boat and staggered the god of thunder. Enraged, Thor mustered all his godly electricity, gripped tight his fishing rod, and dug his heels in so sturdily that both his toes went via the lowest of his boat and into the seabed. Remarkably, the Altuna Runestone even blanketed an outline the foot that went via the planks!

Another exquisite stone is the Hunnestad Monument in Scania, which bears the instance of a girl using a wolf, gripping reins that appear like snakes. The stone has been interpreted to depict the giantess Hyrrokin the "fireplace-wrinkled," who have been summoned to help launch the funeral supply bearing the useless god Baldr.

At least one runestone, the Ledberg stone in Ostergotland, is notion to depict Ragnarok, the mythical doomsday, and the twilight of the Norse gods. The Ledberg stone depicts a huge helmeted warrior presumed to be Odin the All-Father, and gnawing at his heels is a huge beast believed to be Fenrir, the full-size wolf-spawn of Loki, the God of Lies, and who is prophesized to eat Odin throughout the prevent of the place.

Interestingly, there exists a distinct elegance of runestones that had been raised for an altogether unique motive clearly. Heroic boast, or to place it in much less complex phrases, bragging, became tremendously regarded as a virtue in Norse society. The heroes of sagas are regularly portrayed indulging on this dependancy, boasting to crowded mead halls of the monsters that they had slain, the dangers that they had survived and the monuments that they'd built. Indeed, we see that grand boasting is one perpetuated thru many Norsemen of the period: loads of Norsemen, in truth, have had stones carved with the particular reason of immortalizing their private achievements, or even their very personal perceived top notch dispositions. For instance, a runestone at the start positioned in Rasbo, Sweden, is inscribed with textual content that explicitly states that it have been raised with the aid of using someone named "Vigmund, the maximum skillful of men" in his non-public honor, at the equal time as he modified into in spite of the reality that alive. Yet a few one-of-a-kind set of about 20 runestones had been raised at the pleasant of Jarlabanke Ingefastsson, a chieftain who appeared quite keen on leaving his mark at the lands he owned and the bridges and causeways he had built "for his very very personal sake."

As Christianity spread some of the Norsemen, so too did it adjust the testimonies they informed on their runes. In many regions, over 50% of the stone inscriptions encompass a few inference to Christianity; in Uppland, the location wherein may be decided the very first-rate recognition of runic inscriptions within the global, the share rises to approximately 70%. In many times, explicitly Christian trademarks including the pass or prayers were carved into modern-day runestones as later amendments. In reading those runes and their Christian markings, historians are able to piece together the unfold of Christianity in historically Nordic lands. One principle suggests that Uppland became the applicable location at which the war between historical Norse paganism and Christianity first took place. Because the King of Sweden had been newly Christianized, chieftains and specific tribal leaders in Uppland would in all likelihood need to reveal their allegiance by means of using displaying their Christian faith to the area: they did this thru inscribing Christian crosses and prayers to their runestones. Another principle indicates that it changed into definitely a social fashion that extended in reputation some of the clans. The clans of Uppland had been effective, well-established and socially influential; as a quit end result, the Christian markings they found came to be unfold throughout the runestones raised with the useful resource of way of small clans some other place. And as Christianity changed the lifestyle and society of the Norsemen, so too did it trade the memories etched on their runestones: fewer and plenty much less runes emphasized high-quality voyages and celebrated honorable deaths on a ways flung battlefields, or knowledgeable grand testimonies of gods and serpents and the surrender of the area. Instead, later runestones made notes of whether or now not or no longer their subjects have been baptized, or in the event that they were buried in their Christening robes, and regularly even explicitly invoked the figures of Christ, God and the "slight and paradise" of Heaven.

Another manner the runestones confirmed the techniques Christianity changed Nordic society is reflected inside the burial of the lifeless. Since historical instances, Norsemen were frequently buried around runestones, with superb figures interred close to runestones raised of their memory. With the rise of Christianity, the vain had been not buried close to runestones among his ancestors; as an opportunity, their final resting locations were within the cemeteries of local Christian church homes, even though runestones remained famous memorials on the residence.

From the lives of noteworthy, or absolutely privileged Vikings, to the sagas of the gods and mythological figures, to the upward thrust of Christianity, there may be much the runestones have to tell us approximately the subculture of the Viking tribes of Scandinavia. Indeed, their importance to our understanding of the historic Nordic tactics of existence, their deeds, their private characters, their deaths and changing structures of ideals, had been encouraged inside the runor of antique.

Chapter 11: Life Within The Viking Age

In spite in their fearsome reputations as raiders and plunderers, the ordinary Viking have end up a farmer. For most in their lives, the commonplace Viking man and lady cultivated grain vegetation that have been hardy enough to live to tell the story the cold wintry situations, along side barley, rye, and oats. From the discovery of bones, seeds, and different remnants of past food at Viking internet web sites, historians are capable of make knowledgeable guesses approximately the food and drink the Vikings fed on. The annual harvests had been floor as plenty as make flour, porridge, and ale. As nicely, they grew numerous hardy cold weather greens which encompass onions, beans, and cabbages. To complement their healthy dietweight-reduction plan, the Vikings were moreover avid foragers, amassing wild berries and nuts from the close by barren vicinity. And some Vikings moreover stored and raised farm animals which encompass chickens, goats, sheep, pigs, cattle and horses. The livestock furnished eggs, milk, and hundreds-needed manure to help keep the soil fertile. Milk have become used drastically speakme to make cheese and churned into butter, and drank any buttermilk left over from the approaches. Naturally, all through the ones years even as the harvest did not yield enough meals for their families to live on the difficult winters, the Vikings occasionally slaughtered their animals for their meat. The meat grow to be often cooked in a large stew pot over an open fireside, or roasted slowly until crisp and clean over an iron spit. Meat and fish were additionally smoked to dry them for later, and salt changed proper right into a treasured commodity, used within the maintaining of meat and fish and the pickling of vegetables, and modified into generally bought from visiting buyers.

After especially rich harvests or all through auspicious times of the 365 days, Viking settlements frequently loved defensive lavish feasts. During the ones feasts, Vikings have been able to revel in alcoholic drinks which includes ale, a strong drink brewed from roasted barley. More famously, mead come to be the beverage of desire, a drink made through way of fermenting honey with water, and now and again with grains, hops or, inside the occasion that they've been to be had spices and berries. Mead turned into this form of cherished drink and so essential to Viking way of life that it done critical roles of their mythology: one example is the Mead of Poetry, which changed into, steady with legend, brewed from the blood of the god-like being Kvasir. Drinking the Mead of Poetry imbued its imbiber with magical powers, elevating their intelligence and turning them right into a poet or scholar. Beverages have been loved most customarily from wood cups, and on occasion ingesting horns carved from cow horns. Feasts have been often held in birthday celebration of seasonal festivals, which encompass the harvest and midwinter, and throughout funerals. Regardless of the reason for the birthday celebration, feasts have been generally lavish affairs, occasionally lasting over in keeping with week!

As for hotels, we apprehend from the strains of a number of the oldest Viking settlements in spite of the fact that extant that the Norsemen built the partitions in their dwellings out of anything property have been available locally, mainly this come to be timber, stone or compacted blocks of turf. Viking homes were usually prolonged, square container shapes with sloping roofs crafted from dried reeds, thatch or turf. A crude shape of insulation come to be provided with the aid of way of wattle -- this is, a lattice of woven sticks covered in a thick layer of mud to keep out the wind and rain. Most Viking dwellings moreover percentage the identical curious function of their flooring having been dug a sincere distance below ground level; historians theorize that this became finished to assist maintain out draughts from blowing in.

It changed into not unusual for Viking houses to be created from a unmarried room, which became used as communal living quarters shared thru all individuals of the family. Wealthier households, but, could probable boast a small the front corridor, a spacious crucial room, and separated kitchens, bedrooms or possibly hold rooms. Viking villages have been bustling locations in which homes were built near together, crowding a community of winding, slim streets.

Because of the importance of grain farming, which required huge open regions on which to sow fields, Viking cities had been unusual factors of interest in Scandinavia at some stage inside the Viking Age. Only a handful of large Viking settlements dotting the cold, rugged panorama might be taken into consideration towns. An critical feature of Viking townships modified into that they had been nearly entirely located along the shoreline. Not fantastically, the harbor changed into the maximum splendid region in Viking cities, because it have become wherein company issuer and trade boats can also moreover need to effects load and dump their cargo of merchandise and animals. Markets have been often held on the marina, making them the center of exchange. Quays have been additionally often the facilities of the city's business enterprise as well, as shipwrights, clay humans, tanners, leather-primarily based absolutely human beings, carpenters, smiths and other tradesmen often installation their workshops near the harbor to lessen the time, attempt, and consequently rate it took to move their objects and materials.

Within the house itself, furnishings have been scarce, with the normal Viking dwelling house being ready with genuinely a smooth wooden table and benches in which its owners probably every sat and slept on. Perhaps the maximum crucial function of the usual Viking domestic, found in even the poorest dwellings, have become the fireside, an enclosed region wherein the populace must bring together a hearth for heat, illumination, and cooking. But other than the forge belonging to the village blacksmith, dwellings were possibly no longer organized with chimneys: alternatively, houses were geared up with a clean beginning that permit out smoke from the hearth. With no domestic home windows, the interiors of Viking homes had been often dark and gloomy, with mild every so often supplied through the fireside, however extra generally via candles and easy oil lamps.

After a hearty meal of seed porridge and robust barley ale, the regular Viking had no non-public relaxation room to vacate their waste. Most villagers possibly resorted to using a communal rest room -- or cesspit, because the handiest determined with the resource of archaeologists inside the Viking town of Jorvik -- huge holes dug outside, and regularly screened via a fence. As for the bathing, that emerge as accomplished in a timber bucket, or on the nearest drift.

Viking clothes were sewn from spun wool, linen fabric, and animal skins. The clothes worn the ordinary Viking have turn out to be considerably stimulated with the aid of the forms of England, Scotland, and Wales: extended-sleeved tunics and trousers for guys, and prolonged clothing paired with aprons for ladies. During the cold seasons, it turn out to be not unusual for each males and females to put on cloaks, installed thru a brooch. Viking girls generally wore scarves or included their heads with a wrap of material. However, it turn out to be custom for extra more youthful ladies to transport bareheaded. Common footwear blanketed shoes, made truely from tanned or hardened leather-based totally-primarily based. When it entails style enjoy, but, the average Viking dressed to fulfill practical dreams: garments had been there to keep the frame heat! Even so, Viking garments had been not with out their ornamentations. Various natural dyes had been used to coloration fabric: putting blue sun shades have been processed from the woad plant, fantastic reds from madder, and yellow from weld.

In spite of what might be perceived for a flair for practicality, the Vikings have been no longer strictly a sensible humans. Instead, they were professional and capable craftsmen, fashioning many examples of lovable, ornate creations that live on to this modern. Commonly crafted from silver, jet, amber and glass, at the side of close by timber, Viking crafts had been renowned for both their splendor, the complexity of layout and durability. Viking crafts were specifically prized as trade goods with the resource of using one-of-a-kind non-Viking settlements they traded with. Carpenters, blacksmiths, leatherworkers and exclusive craftspeople furthermore supplied the domestic marketplace with the whole lot a Viking needed for each day life: carving timber for ships, shields for the squaddies and toys for the kids; metalworkers cast swords and armor for the berserkers, tools for the farmers and craftsmen, and jewellery for the loads. We apprehend of the excellent and sturdiness of Viking craftsmanship due to the reality a number of their creations live to inform the tale to the present day, loads of years after their advent! From the ones surviving portions, we realize that the Vikings crafted incredible quantities of jewelry in the form of pendants, bracelets, and pins from precious metals, specifically silver. Jewelry changed into worn from valuable metals, frequently as a signal of wealth. Less wealthy human beings wore portions fabricated from a lot much less luxurious bronze or pewter, or silvery alloys. Both men and women to lock cloaks and exclusive garments on the shoulder wore brooches, and necklaces made from glass beads were additionally famous among both genders. Common motifs found in jewelry, woodcarvings, and longships depict animals which includes wolves and mythological figures which include dragons.

As we are capable of see from studies of their settlements and dwellings, the Vikings have been not often barbaric raiders and pillagers who relied on plundering neighboring villages for his or her meals, wealth, and livelihood. Even even though the mere point out of the phrase 'Viking' these days inspires the photograph of a frenzied warrior adorned in chainmail and wading into battle after high-quality struggle, the truth became that the each day life of the commonplace Viking changed into, for the more a part of the three hundred and sixty five days, alternatively everyday of early agricultural civilizations of the time. That is, their lives have been ruled by way of manner of manner of a rigorous and annual time table of sowing, tending and harvesting their fields, cooking, drying, salting, smoking and pickling food, tanning leather-based-based, smithing and forging the smooth iron equipment they used, or dyeing and scouring textiles used to tailor their garments. With technological traits much like the windmill and advanced metallurgy still as a minimum a century away, the Vikings relied on handiest their fingers and essential tools to supply them with the manner they needed to live on. Daily lifestyles, then, emerge as a war in opposition to the tough realities of finding enough food and safe haven for clearly all of us in the community.

Chapter 12: Vikings At War

But make no mistake; the Vikings have been proud warriors who belonged to a warrior way of life. According to historical life-style, proudly owning weapons modified into no longer first-rate a privilege given to all loose Norse guys however a social obligation. So, essential have been a Viking's weapon and warrior manner of lifestyles that the consumer god of all Vikings, Odin the All-father, is himself quoted as having stated, "Don't depart your weapons mendacity approximately inside the again of your again in a topic; you in no way recognize on the equal time as you could need all of a surprising your spear." Indeed, neighboring peoples rightly feared the wrath of Viking raiders who prowled the coasts and delivery lanes, on occasion ranging far and massive from their a long way flung location of beginning.

As war and struggle have been supposedly the most prestigious hobby for a Viking to engage in, it stands to reason that a Viking's social fame decided the armaments he wore and carried into conflict. Wealthy Vikings adorned themselves with a spear, a massive spherical wood guard, and probable a sword. Swords were mainly prized as popularity symbols often passed down from father to son, with the sagas regularly claiming that they were imbued with magic powers. And pleasant the very richest Vikings may additionally need to find out the money for to equip themselves with a helmet. Other forms of armor had been pretty uncommon and is perception to have seen constrained use most effective among Viking the Aristocracy, or in particular fearsome professional warriors. Vikings of decrease social reputation, which include farmers, often armed themselves with best a spear, a guard, a common ax or seax, a shape of huge knife. Some also can have delivered alongside their searching bows and hired them to whittle down an enemy rate at some level inside the hole degrees of combat engagements.

Armor

Only nobles may also need to come up with the coins for to equip themselves with armor in the shape of an iron helmet and a chainmail tunic. Contrary to famous perception, the most remarkable function of Viking helmets changed into not, usually, ornamental horns or wings festooned on every problem of the helmet. (Historians credit score this famous and enduring false impression of Vikings sporting horned or winged helmets to nineteenth century Romanticism.) Indeed, Viking helmets have been no longer usually horned. Instead, Viking helmets have been frequently built with robust guards at some stage in the eyes and over the nose, for a similarly layer of protection. Because of their shortage, helmets have been regularly lavishly adorned as a show of its owner’s wealth. Not ones to underestimate their private protection, some poorer Vikings ought to outfit themselves in helmets crafted from hardened leather-based-based totally-based. To guard their hands and torsos, Viking chainmail become a form of armor home crafted from plenty of interlocking iron earrings and served to deflect slashing attacks which includes those from sword cuts or blows from an ax.

Shields

In a Viking's arsenal, shields have been the maximum commonplace shape of protection from physical damage, forming the primary (and for plenty Vikings the best) line of safety.

The most common form of Viking shields changed into the spherical shield. Famous Viking sagas specifically factor out that linden emerge as the preferred timber for crafting shields, in spite of the reality that shields excavated from Viking gravesites show that fir, alder, and poplar have been greater extensively utilized in common exercising. These specific timbers have been specifically selected to be now not very dense, therefore mild-weight and maneuverable. The houses of fir, alder, and poplar moreover made them now not going to splinter and spoil, not like denser, heavier woods like oak. When a Viking guard did necessarily yield to the strain of a blow, their fibers of those particular timbers had a dishonest to snag spherical blades and prevented an attacker from reducing any deeper, not with out substantially extra pressure. In addition, Viking shields had been regularly strengthened with leather or every now and then iron throughout the rim. Some shields had a strong metal center known as a md, which provided enough and treasured safety for the wielder's hand and lessened the threat of the defend-bearer being disarmed or losing his shield from the wonder of impact. Round shields varied appreciably in length from 18" - 48" (45 - a hundred twenty cm) in diameter, with with the resource of some distance the most commonplace shields starting from 30" - 36" (75 - 90 cm).

A commonplace warfare tactic most of the Vikings have end up known as the guard wall or skjaldborg, the precept formation in which warriors could probably endure their shields and stand aspect via factor. In doing so, the infantrymen created a line of interlocked shields to thrust back enemy enhance and missile hearth. By thrusting their spears at their enemies, the shield wall come to be additionally a frightening assault formation, allowing the Vikings to batter relentlessly closer to the the the the front ranks in their enemies. Another famous tactic changed into the svinfylking or the "boar snout." In this tactic, warriors could acquire right right into a wedge formation, with the fiercest and satisfactory-equipped warriors forming the give up of the wedge. The boar snout would then charge headlong into enemy ranks, thrusting, stabbing and cutting until that they had burst via the the front line of their enemies.

Archaeological findings have discovered to us that each Viking warrior valued their shields quite. Round shields were often embellished with complex designs, and every now and then instead ornate silver and gold metalwork had been implemented across the boss and anchors for the straps. Interestingly, there can be an entire subgenre of Skaldic poetry called "protect poems," which describe landscapes, styles, scenes and designs famously painted on shields. One specifically noteworthy skaldic poem entails us from the late 9th century, the Ragnarsdrapa, and describes how some Vikings may want to beautify their scenes depicting mythological scenes regarding the wartime exploits of the gods of Valhalla. The Gokstad deliver, probable the most famous recovered seafaring vessel from the Viking Age, has locations on its hull railings for shields to be hung and fixed. It emerge as believed that, even as mounted this way on a supply's hull, the shields served to protect the supply's crews from freezing waves and buffeting winds on the identical time as out on the immoderate seas, and there may additionally additionally were religious, or superstitious significance to decorating one's craft with the shields of its occupants.

Fairly presently, it emerge as recommended that Vikings also used a 2d kind of protect: the kite guard, a big, almond common protect that changed into rounded on the top and curved all of the way right right down to a tapered issue at the lowest. The name "kite shield" refers back to the guard's precise shape, which pretty resembles a flying kite. To current-day historians, kite shields are carefully related to Norman battle, however it's been proposed that the Normans inherited the kite protect format from the Vikings. To date, however, there has been no archaeological evidence in guide of this concept.

The Spear

Contrary to modern day assumptions, the maximum not unusual weapon of the Viking hordes have become no longer the conflict ax, but the spear. Spears had been most often utilized by the Scandinavian peasant beauty, which fashioned the bulk of the rank and document of Viking armies. Throwing spears were used substantially with the useful useful resource of Viking warriors, and references to spears inside the palms of Vikings had been made in almost each surviving report of Viking raids. Capable of being thrown as a ranged weapon, similarly to slashing and thrusting, spears have been nicely relevant to their formations and techniques, which required a high diploma of mobility and adapting to changing battlefield conditions. The normal Viking spear have end up made from a metal spearhead with a pointy blade established to a hollow wood shaft about 2 to three meters in duration. Spearheads themselves want to diploma among an imposing 20 - 60 cm, with longer spearheads performing inside the latter years of the Viking Age. The sagas element out a particularly famend shape of spear referred to as the krokspjot, or 'hooked spears,' whereas a few broader headed spears were called hoggspjot, or 'cutting spears,' and had been hired for cutting and slashing. Not as a substitute, barbed thrown spears often sported fewer ornamentation that thrusting spears, as thrown spears frequently pass unretrieved after they leave the thrower's hand. Thrown spears often boasted lighter, narrower spearheads just so they may be thrown farther and with more accuracy, on the identical time as spears with heavier, broader blades were utilized in thrusting and closer variety skirmishes. Spearheads had been usually fastened securely to the shaft with a pin; in a few sagas, a few characters are defined pulling out the pin and casting away the spearhead to prevent a foe from claiming and the usage of their favored guns.

In addition to their versatility, probably the leader motive inside the lower back of the spear's popularity is that it is able to be made with inferior metallic, and everyday far a whole lot much less steel than specific guns, which incorporates a sword. Naturally, this made spears a miles extra low cost desire, and additional correctly available, as it have become in all likelihood that even a common blacksmith need to craft spears without any specialised functionality or schooling. In spite of its enchantment to the poorer training, Vikings fostered a deep spiritual attachment to the spear: a paranormal spear named Gungnir come to be the signature weapon of Odin, king of all Norse gods and the god of battle. One saga, the Eyrbyggja saga, describes a custom of throwing a spear proper over the enemy navy preceding to the start of a conflict: this spear changed into speculated to guarantee victory thru claiming it for Odin.

The Battle Axe

A near second to the spear, the ax became the diverse maximum commonplace hand weapons used by Viking warriors. Because of the prohibitive cost concerned in making swords, many Vikings armed themselves with an ax. Axes are so regular in archeological web sites that historians can draw the belief that it determined huge use no longer definitely as a weapon, but a not unusual tool for normal use. This principle is supported with the useful resource of the discovery of axes in the graves of both Viking women and men.

Several sorts of big axes had been specialised for use in warfare. These ‘war axes’ had massive heads and longer shafts for stepped forward gain and harm dealing capacity. The maximum famous of these styles of conflict axes, the Dane Axes, had been as long as someone and had been made to be wielded with every fingers. Some ax heads have been inlaid with silver designs, and because the Viking Age advanced and melee battle advanced, war axes began out out to interest more and more crescent original edges measuring as lots as forty five cm (18 inches). These axes were called breioox, or "large axes." Viking axes were normally ready with only a single bit; the well-known modern photograph of a double-bitted Viking ax are probable natural fable.

Still, Viking conflict axes had been in fact devastating guns. Sturdy enough to be swung or thrown, the normal Viking ax packed enough of a punch to sever limbs, splinter shields and split heads. Among the axes most feared for their deadliness became the Mammen Axe, which became ideally fitted for throwing and melee combat.

Though ax blades have been typically made from wrought iron with a metallic decreasing aspect and consequently have been lots much less highly-priced to offer than a sword, many Vikings grew linked to their weapons of choice. Like many one-of-a-kind quantities of Scandinavian weaponry, axes have been frequently given names; in line with the Prose Edda, as documented with the aid of Snorri Sturluson, axes frequently carried the names of giant beings, like she-trolls.

The Knifr and the Seax

Two extremely good styles of knives have been used by the Vikings. By a ways the greater not unusual knife, referred to as a knifr, have end up built more it appears that evidently, and has been found in most Viking graves. Even slaves, girls and kids had been buried with the knifr tey owned. Knifr had been used as normal software system, even as longer and broader bladed versions have been likely utilized in looking and fight.

The other type of knife changed into the 'damaged-decrease once more style seax.' The seax modified into usually heavier than a ordinary knife and turn out to be used commonly as a machete or falchion. Wealthier Viking guys may also additionally own massive seax, some massive sufficient to be correctly wielded like a sword. A seax had a single location and heavy blade and seemed, in stylish, to be as an alternative of a crude weapon. This supposed they had been smooth to use and bring as compared to a ordinary sword. It grow to be likely that small seaxes were possibly in the abilties of a not unusual blacksmith to put together.

Having loved exceptional use by using the usage of the Saxons, the seax design have become inherited with the aid of the Vikings settling in England and Ireland but seem very rarely in Scandinavia.

The Viking Sword

A sword within the Viking age was designed for use in a unmarried hand, located with the aid of a defend. They have been double-edged, with a blade length of as a lot as ninety cm. In form and layout, the Viking sword drew cautiously from the masses in advance Roman spatha: it had an terrific grip, no wonderful cross-protect, and a protracted deep fuller.

Swords have been prohibitively expensive to make, and for that reason, proudly proudly owning a sword have become a sign of wealth and immoderate popularity. One Viking saga, the Laxdaela saga, mentions that a selected sword have emerge as worth half a crown, that have end up an amount capable of buying an entire herd of sixteen milk cows. Scabbards were timber, advantageous in leather-primarily based and worn in a strap all through the right shoulder. Early Viking swords had been forged using a method called sample welding, which worried time and again twisting and melding strips of iron and slight metallic to supply a sturdy blade and hardened problem. Later Viking swords had been made absolutely from a unmarried shape of metal, believed to be imported from the Rhineland. The sword grip modified into commonly crafted from a non-metal organic cloth, together with timber, horn or antler, after which wrapped spherical with material for a more comfortable grip -- alas, because of this few Viking sword hilts live on to be found thru cutting-edge archaeological efforts. Because of each the know-how and charge required to craft a sword, Viking blades have been frequently inlaid with makers' marks and inscriptions, on the facet of the 'INGELRII' or 'VLFBERHT' determined on recovered blades from the duration. Craftsmen frequently delivered their very personal inventive touches inside the shape of elaborately decorated hilts, and plenty of swords have been given names that emphasized their deadliness or extremely good appearances, which incorporates Leg-biter and Gold-hilt.

Owning a sword intended a Viking-owned a immoderate degree of personal and familial honor. Swords were believed to be bequeathed with magical powers and a 'lifestyles' of its private and changed into passed down from father to son. The older the sword, regularly the extra it improved in cost. There has been proof from an examination of Viking burial net websites that sometimes, the swords belonging to specially wealthy warriors have been 'killed' in advance than they had been buried with their proprietors. 'Killing' a sword involved bending or twisting the blade simply so it became unusable. Apart from the feasible ritualistic importance of retiring a weapon with its wielder, killing a sword also served to discourage grave robbers from traumatic the burial internet website online an awesome way to thieve the sort of exceedingly-prized weapons.

Chapter 13: Viking Mythology

We understand from severa belongings which include medieval manuscripts, archaeological findings, and folks way of life that the Norsemen had a rich and complex mythology. The Prose Edda and the Poetic Edda are arguably of the maximum important equipment for our information of Norse mythology: written greater frequently than no longer inside the 13th century through Snorri Sturulson and severa nameless authors, this manuscript collects in the text the rich oral manner of lifestyles as advocated with the aid of phrase of mouth, kennings, and skaldic poetry.

Viking myths describe the deeds and adventures of an elaborate pantheon of deities. Stemming from historic Norse paganism and enduring prolonged after the Christianization of Scandinavia, Norse mythology is rich with large than life heroes and terrific beings.

Thor, Champion of the Gods

Central to the surviving debts of Norse mythology are the plights and deeds of the gods. While severa gods are referred to inside the supply texts, by using manner of way of far the most famous god a number of the Scandinavians within the path of the Viking Age have grow to be Thor. Often associated with thunder, lightning, storms, very welltrees strength, hallowing and fertility, Thor is a herculean figure devoted to the protection of mankind. With fierce eyes, fiery hair and a fire-purple beard, Thor is the son of the god Odin and the husband of the golden-haired goddess Sif. Thor's maximum important signature weapon is Mjölnir, depicted in Norse mythology as one of the most fearsome guns inside the cosmos, capable of leveling whole mountains with a unmarried blow. Its call meaning "grinder" or "crusher," Mjölnir modified into purportedly crafted by using way of dwarves, and it end up a mishap at some stage in its advent that induced its in the fundamental short manage. Among

Thor's unique magical possessions is his belt Megingjörð, which doubles his already prodigious strength, his iron gloves Járngreipr, and the lifestyles-giving staff Gríðarvölr. Thor rode into warfare in a chariot pulled with the resource of black goats, Tanngrisnir and Tanngnjóstr, which he slaughters and eats for sustenance, and then resurrects.

Many of Thor's exploits contain him the usage of into fierce battles and relentlessly slaughtering his foes, or finding out his mettle through difficult a particularly volatile opponent. In the comedic poem Þrymskviða, Mjöllnir is stolen through the jötunn Þrymr, who publicizes that the hammer will only be back if the goddess Freyja is delivered to him as his wife. Not as an alternative, even as asked, Freyja pointedly refuses and storms out of the hall, and in her rage drops her famed necklace Brisingamen. After a few talk, the gods contrive a plan to ship Thor in region of

Freyja, through dressing him from head to toe in lavish jewels, a veiled bridal headdress, women's clothes that go along with the go with the flow all of the way all the way down to his knees, and Freyja's trademark necklace Brisingamen. In spite of his preliminary protests, Thor unhappily goes collectively with the plan and, joined through his trickster brother Loki, the 2 stress to Jötunheimr, the frozen kingdom of the jötun. There, they'll be greeted by Þrymr, who has put together a lavish feast. Thor ferociously beverages and eats, consuming complete animals and three entire casings of mead. Þrymr reveals this behavior at odds together with his expectancies of Freyja, but Loki, in the guise of "a totally clever maid," makes the excuse that Freyja's urge for meals is because of her having fasted for 8 complete days in advance than their arrival due to her eagerness to fulfill her new husband. When Þrymr lifts Freyja's veil in an try to kiss her, he's greeted thru the sight of terrifying eyes staring again at him, eyes apparently burning with fireside. Again, Loki perpetuates the ruse through claiming that Freyja's eyes exquisite seem that manner because she hasn't slept for 8 nights in her eagerness. Finally, the jötnar deliver out Mjöllnir to "sanctify the bride" and lay it on her lap, simply so Þrymr and "Freyja" can be wed. Upon seeing his cherished hammer, Thor laughs internally, then proper away takes maintain of the weapon, movements Þrymr, brutally beats all the jötnar, and so gets his hammer lower once more.

On one journey, Thor goes fishing for whales and makes a decision to bait his line with the top of an ox. The massive serpent Jörmungandr takes the hook. Using his exceptional energy, Thor pulls the serpent on board and violently slams him inside the head together together with his hammer. The struggle, however the serpent possibly escapes lower returned into the water. Thor consoles himself with the useful resource of wearing numerous whales once more to shore.

One noteworthy exception to the same old Thor narratives can be discovered inside the Hárbarðsljóð, Odin, probably searching for to mood his son's heat-headedness, disguises himself as a ferryman and arranges to be met with the aid of way of Thor all through his travels "from the east." Thor, upon encountering the ferryman at an inlet, tries to hail a journey. The ferryman refuses and is right away rude and obnoxious to Thor. At first, Thor manages to hold his tongue, but the ferryman keeps to barb him and grows extra competitive. The poem then becomes a flying healthy, a raucous but poetic alternate of insults, among Thor and the ferryman in which it is discovered that in his time "in the east", Thor had slain several jötnar and an entire island of berzerk ladies. At the belief in their trade, Thor does no longer, in truth, offer in to his rage, however rather brushes off the ferryman and ultimately ends up strolling throughout the inlet as a substitute.

Thor’s lack of lifestyles is foretold to arise in the route of Ragnarok, the mythical battle of the gods and the give up of the universe. There, Thor will another time conflict with the remarkable Midgard Serpent Jörmungandr, and although he'll manage to slay the beast, Thor will take no extra than 9 steps earlier than succumbing to its venom, “sinking fearlessly” into the palms of the earth.

Odin, Wise, and Noble

Another god stated numerous times in the source texts is Odin. Widely reputable in Norse mythology, Odin is a determine of both warlike and scholarly importance, associated with recovery, loss of life, the Aristocracy, know-how and scholarly interests, warfare strategies and battle, justice and judgment, sorcery, poetry and highbrow pastimes. It is important to word that Odin has been reputable thru the Germanic peoples in the course of their data, lengthy in advance than the upward push of the Viking Age. In Old English, he have become called Wōden and in Old High German as Wuotan or Wōtan. In areas traditionally inhabited via historic Germanic peoples, many area names go through references to Odin. Even in modern-day-day English, the day of the week Wednesday bears his name. While a remarkable deal of the sooner peoples' model of Odin has been out of location to time, our clearest expertise of Odin comes from the preserved Old Norse works.

In surviving Old Norse texts which includes the Prose Edda, Odin is often portrayed as having a long beard and simplest one eye. He is often visible carrying a cloak and a tremendous hat, and frequently wielding his famed spear Gungnir. Various animal partners often accompany Odin on his travels: the wolves Geri and Freki, and the ravens Huginn and Muninn act as his scouts and brings him statistics and facts from anywhere inside the mortal realm of Midgard. In warfare, Odin rides on a flying, 8-legged steed referred to as Sleipnir through the sky into the underworld. Also known as the 'All-Father,' Odin is attested as having many sons, most famously the god Baldr. Odin is likewise credited with having taken a exquisite element inside the arrival of the world via using using slaying the primordial being Ymir, and granting the gift of existence to the number one humans Ask and Embla. In some texts, Odin is given a selected association with Yule, and he is likewise credited with bringing every runes and poetry to the mortal worldwide. Driven with the beneficial aid of an irrepressible thirst for expertise, Odin is keen on touring the worlds attempting to find increasingly understanding, at times in hide -- maximum famously with the useful resource of obtaining the Mead of Poetry

In Old Norse texts, Odin has command over the all-girl valkyries, who fly over web web sites of first rate battles searching for honorable souls to welcome into Valhalla. Odin gets half of of of those who die in war; the ones welcomed into Valhalla are referred to as the einherjar, and are encouraged to eat and drink their fill at the identical time as getting prepared each day for the sports of Ragnarok, the very last high-quality warfare they will be destined to combat. In later folklore, Odin seems due to the fact the leader of the Wild Hunt, a procession of ghostly hunters the usage of throughout the wintry weather sky visible as an omen foretelling conflict, loss of life or disaster.

Odin's loss of life is foretold inside the poem Völuspá, which recounts Odin's conversations with an undead völva, a shaman or smart female. The völva imparts to Odin (and, thereby, the readers) attention from a while past, collectively with how Odin and considered one of a kind gods gave lifestyles to the primary people, Ask and Embla, and helped them continue to exist via granting them the three gadgets thru the three gods: Sense, Blood, and Spirit. After Odin brings her a trove of bejeweled necklaces, the völva goes immediately to impart more understanding, which embody Odin's function as leader and hero of the number one warfare of the sector: the conflict the various Vanir and the Aesir, disparate agencies of gods who vied for dominion over the mortal realm of Midgard. In her storytelling, the völva eventually foretells of Odin's destined death at Ragnarok. On that battlefield, Odin will fight in competition to the large wolf Fenrir, who has grown so large that he is going to understand Odin in his jaws and swallow him entire. One of Odin's sons, Víðarr, will avenge his father via stabbing the wolf inside the coronary coronary heart. After the arena is burned and swept away thru a flood, first-class to rise anew as a lush and verdant paradise, the surviving gods and mortals will meet and maintain in thoughts Odin's deeds and bear in mind his "historical runes."

Freyja, the Beautiful

Another popular figure in Norse mythology is Freyja, a goddess frequently associated with intercourse, fertility, beauty and love, wealth, battle, and loss of life. Among Freyja's most prized possessions is Brisingamen, that is at instances portrayed as a necklace or a torc, a shape of thick neck-ring, and is alluded to as being filigreed, lavishly bejeweled, and amber or golden in shade. Freyja moreover owned a cloak of falcon feathers, capable of granting flight to its wearer, rode on a chariot pulled by using cats, and keeps her loved boar Hildisvini thru her aspect.

Freyja is so effective and influential that she is stated to say half of of of of those warriors who fell in struggle; the other half may visit Odin's hall Valhalla. Freyja's afterlife changed right right into a heavenly subject known as Folkvangr, and there resided her hall Sessrúmnir, which modified into "huge and incredible." In the sagas and poems, Freyja is frequently invoked in topics of fertility and love, assists one of a kind deities by using lending them her falcon-feathered cloak, and her setting splendor makes her a common target for kidnappings, generally at the fingers of effective jötnar seeking to make her their accomplice. Freyja's husband, the "frenzied" and wanderlust god Óðr, is often absent from domestic. Freyja laments their distance with the useful resource of crying tears of crimson gold for him and every so often is going on her non-public adventures searching for him.

Several plants nearby to the Vikings' place of foundation have been as soon as named after Freyja, consisting of Freyja's hair and Freyja's tears. However, at some degree in the end end result of Christianity, the selection of the goddess changed into changed with that of the Virgin Mary.

Loki, the Father of Monsters

At once every antagonist and best friend to the gods of Valhalla, and each god and jötunn, the trickster Loki is the father of Hel, the wolf Fenrir, and the sector serpent Jörmungandr. A proficient shapeshifter, Loki is likewise the mother of the 8-legged, sky-faring horse Sleipner.

Loki's complicated, tough, and at times contradicting dating with the alternative Norse gods varies via deliver. At instances, Loki is described as supporting the gods on their adventures, while at others, behaves in a malicious way closer to them. Loki's super guile and penchant for trickery is aided by means of the truth that he's a shapeshifter, having assumed the form of a salmon, an are, a seal, a fly, and an aged female.

Ultimately, Loki is solid out thru the gods and condemned as a villain, an act seen as the first in the complex chain of sports that result in the destruction of the vicinity and the Norse gods at Ragnarok. The sports that caused this future begins offevolved offevolved with Baldr, the an lousy lot-loved son of Odin and his partner, the goddess Frigg. After waking from a dream of his very personal demise, Baldr grow to be a bargain depressed and confided his desires to his mother. Frigg, recognized for her extensive understanding of factors beyond and subjects however to go returned, has moreover suffered similar dreams of her son's untimely lack of life. Because Baldr turn out to be an lousy lot cherished, Frigg used her big strength to command every object in all the nation-states to in no manner harm Baldr. And all gadgets made this vow besides mistletoe, a plant which Frigg had placed too 'more younger' to be sworn into a binding oath.

Upon taking note of of this, Loki, ever the maker of mischief, trendy a magical spear out of mistletoe. He then moved speedy to the vicinity wherein the gods have been reveling of their new-located hobby: hurling devices to Baldr, simplest to examine them ricochet off of him with out harming him. Loki exceeded a spear to the blind god Höðr, who flung it. Guided through using Loki's magic, the spear fatally pierced Baldr, killing him in which he stood, to the horror of the on searching gods.

Baldr have become ceremonially burnt to loss of existence on his deliver, Hringhorni, the most important of all of the ships. In some versions, Nanna, Baldr's spouse, turned into so triumph over with grief that she threw herself onto the funeral hearth to look at for Ragnarok while she might be reunited in conjunction with her husband. Baldr's horse, with all his trappings, end up moreover burned at the pyre. It emerge as said that Hringhorni modified into so laden with treasure and parting devices from the gods that the giantess Hyrrokin needed to be summoned to push it out to sea. Borne on a good sized wolf, Hyrrokin top notch barely controlled the feat, mustering a lot stress that hearth flashed from the rollers and all of the earth shook due to the truth the funeral barge released out to sea.

Unable to allow pass of her loved son, Frigg made many entreaties to Hel, goddess of the underworld realm that bore her call. So passionate were Frigg's pleas that Hel changed into ultimately swayed, as a minimum, relatively. Hel struck a bargain with Frigg: if all items alive and vain wept for Baldr, Hel should release Baldr from the underworld. And all did weep for Baldr the Beautiful... except for a giantess, frequently presumed to be the god Loki in hide. Other variations have Loki casting a spell upon the Willow tree, which changed into once tall and proud. This spell avoided the Willow from weeping for Baldr. After the Willow changed into released from the spell, the tree bowed deeply in its grief, and from then on, have become certain to weep steadily.

When Loki's role in engineering the murder of Baldr have turn out to be unraveled, the gods were quick to proper their revenge. Loki became captured and lashed to the aspect of a cliff, certain with the entrails of one among his sons. In the Poetic Edda and the Prose Edda, the goddess of the quest, Skaði, locations a serpent above Loki's head -- the serpent's fangs always drip venom that Loki's spouse Sigyn want to gather right into a bowl. However, she want to drain the bowl while it is entire; inside the interim, the venom that drips onto Loki's head motives pain so excruciating that his writhings had been said to motive earthquakes. At the onset of Ragnarok, Loki is foretold to slip unfastened from his bounds and lead an military of jötnar to the apocalyptic battlegrounds. There, he's going to do struggle with the god Heimdallr, and from that confrontation, the two will slay each unique.

Chapter 14: The Viking Empire At Its Height

The Vikings are probable one of the maximum feared and faulty civilizations to emerge inside the route of the Medieval length. Originating from Scandinavia, they first appeared in Britain in the latter a part of the 8th century CE, when they commenced to attack through manner of and large undefended monasteries, plundering them of all their valuables.

Various massive Scandinavian settlements had been set up within the course of Britain with the useful resource of the usage of the latter a part of the 9th century, attaining political manipulate over a giant location of america. By the flip of the eleventh century, Britain have become dominated with the resource of the Danish king, similarly to numerous invasions via Harald Hardrada, the king of Norway, and William, referred to as William the Bastard, the Duke of Normandy, who grow to be a descendant of the Vikings who had settled within the north of France.

However, the maximum critical part of this time become the oblique consequences of Viking have an effect on and interference within British politics and society, the arrival of Scotland and England, freshly unified territories. Although the Vikings had established themselves inside their home u . S ., the height in their power and have an effect on have become sincerely among the 8th and twelfth centuries, after they unfold across Europe and the Middle East, entering into touch with various one in all a type cultures.

The beginning of the Vikings in Britain begins offevolved in 793 while Alcuin of York penned a letter to Higbald, the bishop of Lindisfarne and King Ethelred of

Northumbria, lamenting approximately an unanticipated assault on Lindisfarne monastery from the Viking pillagers, who've been maximum likely a set of sailors from Norway crusing to Northumbria. This letter, which despite the fact that survives, suggests that the monastery became no longer devastated, however, Alciun does suggest that destiny attacks may be averted by way of way of moral reforms within the monastery.

Numerous different monasteries had been attacked and destroyed in northern Britain with the resource of way of the Viking raiders, together with any information or files that described those attacks. Although we do not have any surviving historical statistics of those assaults in Scotland, archaeologists trust that the harm the Vikings did emerge as huge.

In 802 CE, fireplace destroyed Iona, with 68 monks perishing during a further raid only four years later. The clergymen who survived escaped to Kells (in County Meath in Ireland), taking with them a gospel e-book; this e-book is called the Book of Kells, but modified into maximum probably created in Iona.

Countless monasteries at some point of northern England and Scotland were worn out, without any trace within the historical information. The priests deserted Lindisfarne, but they journeyed across the north of England with the remains of St. Cuthbert, and in the long run settled in Durham in 995.

Due to the critically limited historical writings of the time, it is tough to make certain as to how hundreds of an have an impact at the Vikings did to Scotland. However, it's miles apparent that the Norwegian settlers had a extremely good impact in Sutherland, Caithness, and the Shetland and Orkney Islands because of the numerous area names which may be despite the fact that used these days.

The Vikings who settled in Scotland at this era are, in step with a super range of historians and archaeologists, believed to have been responsible for the vanishing of the Pict kingdom. The Picts, at some stage in the 8th century, had been one of the most huge and valuable kingdoms in the u.S.. However, thru using the latter part of the ninth century, they had disappeared. The Scottish country had changed them, who've been the descendants of Irish settlers who had arrived in Scotland at some point of the 5th and 6th centuries.

Particularly beneath the manipulate of King Cinaed mac Alpin (additionally referred to as Kenneth MacAlpine), the Scots started to promote themselves due to the fact the rulers of absolutely everyone in Alba, or northern Britain, the use of the Vikings' presence as an competitive and practical method.

By weaving and inventing severa participants of the own family a few of the

Pict and the Scottish kingdoms, the latest rulers started to set up a brand new country wide statistics. They moreover began out to promote the belief that the promoter of these living on this region modified into the founder of the monastery at Iona, St. Columba.

Until spherical 840, raids in northern England with the useful useful resource of the Vikings remained sporadic, but thru way of the following decade, they had started out staying longer. By 860, the Vikings had been sending large forces to Britain, truely determined to overcome this new land.

In 865, the Vikings had enforced the East Angles within the south to useful useful resource them in offering an arm. By the subsequent year, this military turn out to be able to take control of York. In 867, they took the south of the Northumbrian state.

www.ingramcontent.com/pod-product-compliance
Lightning Source LLC
Chambersburg PA
CBHW070951120726
47910CB00004B/1198

* 9 7 8 0 9 9 5 3 3 2 4 6 1 *